LOGAN MARTIN

JOURNEY TO GOLD

OLYMPIC GOLD ∗ X-GAMES GOLD ∗ WORLD CHAMPION

LOGAN MARTIN

JOURNEY TO GOLD

LOGAN MARTIN WITH **SCOTT GULLAN**

PENGUIN BOOKS

UK | USA | Canada | Ireland | Australia
India | New Zealand | South Africa | China

Penguin Books is part of the Penguin Random House group of companies whose
addresses can be found at global.penguinrandomhouse.com

Penguin
Random House
Australia

First published by Penguin Books in 2022

Copyright © Logan Martin, 2022

The moral right of the author has been asserted.

Front cover photograph courtesy Wayne Cant
Cover design by Luke Causby/Blue Cork
Internal design and typesetting by Midland Typesetters, Australia

Printed and bound in Australia by Griffin Press, an accredited
ISO AS/NZS 14001 Environmental Management Systems printer

A catalogue record for this
book is available from the
National Library of Australia

ISBN 978 0 14377 825 7

penguin.com.au

We at Penguin Random House Australia acknowledge that Aboriginal and Torres Strait
Islander peoples are the Traditional Custodians and the first storytellers of the lands
on which we live and work. We honour Aboriginal and Torres Strait Islander peoples'
continuous connection to Country, waters, skies and communities. We celebrate
Aboriginal and Torres Strait Islander stories, traditions and living cultures;
and we pay our respects to Elders past and present.

This book is dedicated to my amazing dad, Sean – my biggest believer and forever supporter. I will do everything I can to continue making you proud. I know you'll be watching down on me. Rest easy, Dad. I love you. (1963–2022)

And to my son, Noah, and daughter, Luna – there are no words to describe the amount of love I have for you. I hope this book reminds you that you can do anything you set your mind to as long as you put in the work. Reach for the stars and you might just become one!

CONTENTS

* Because I don't do 13.

1
LEARNING TO FLY

I always wanted to tackle the big kids.

Someone told me once that the best way to tackle an opponent on the Rugby League field was to take out their legs, because then they couldn't run. That was instantly wired into my brain, so from that moment on, every time I'd make a tackle, I'd take the legs. And I'd do it even though I was the smallest player on the field. In fact, that was almost my badge of honour: I never let my height, or lack thereof, stop me from doing anything.

It was like a chip on my shoulder. It made me even more determined to show people that I could do things.

From the age of six, when I first started playing rugby, that was my attitude. You'd often see kids too scared to go at the big kids, but I threw caution to the wind and didn't seem to care about what happened. I just went at them. Take the legs.

It was an attitude that would serve me well, although, despite my love for the game, Rugby League didn't turn out to be my sport.

I grew up in Logan City, Queensland – yes, I was named after the place, but more about that later – and played with three junior clubs around the area, beginning with Waterford before moving to Logan Brothers, which was famous for producing many NRL stars, including one of the greatest of all time, Melbourne Storm's Cameron Smith.

I played as a hooker because my ball control and awareness on the field was good. At my third club, Beenleigh, we had an above-average team that made the local grand final, but then a new coach came on board and I found myself on the outer as he played favourites with his son and some of the Islander boys.

The smallest kid was always the first to go, no matter how good they were in junior teams. I was only getting on for five minutes here and there before being benched again. I didn't want to be a part of that, and my parents agreed, so at the age of twelve my Rugby League career was over.

Despite this setback, playing sports was my passion, and it would come as no surprise to learn that my favourite class at school was HPE (Health and Physical Education). That's the one class where I'd listen intently to the teacher and always do my best to impress them. I was a dynamo at school sports; I seemed to be able to pick up different sports quite quickly. My motivation was simple, even back then: I just wanted to be better than everyone else. Whether that was in the swimming pool or even on the gymnastics floor, I wanted to be the best.

This desire to be the centre of attention on the sporting field was ironic in a way because generally I was a shy kid who didn't have too much to say. But there was something about being good at sport that gave me an identity. For some reason I always felt like people expected that I would be good. There was actually no reason for me to think that way. It might sound crazy, but in my mind I wanted to prove that to be right. The problem was, with rugby out, I needed to fill that void.

The unexpected solution came when my parents moved us into a new rental on Augusta Street, Crestmead.

My brother, Nathan, was a year older, and I was your typical annoying younger brother, following him everywhere. Every now and then he'd go down to a local skatepark and ride his BMX around. That was my first introduction to the sport.

Our new house in Crestmead was just a block away from the park, which was a magnet for young teenage boys wanting to hang out. Nathan was quickly drawn in, with his little brother always a step behind. Obviously I needed to look the part, so for my next birthday I asked for a BMX of my own.

My first bike was a small 16-inch frame ABD green machine, and the day after I got it Dad, Nathan and I went down to the skatepark. Next to all the ramps was some grassy park area, and I was riding around there when I crashed. I'd turned too fast and put it in the dirt, but the problem wasn't what happened to me – it was the massive scratch I'd just put on my new bike.

I was devastated. I couldn't believe I'd ruined my pride and joy on one of the very first rides. Time healed that wound, and soon I was going down with Nathan all the time to ride in the park.

The Crestmead Skate Park had a little bit of everything for BMX riders and skaters. There was a round bowl; a cornered, three-sided bowl; quarter-pipes; a half-pipe; stairs; rails; a fun box; ledges; pyramids and big banks.

It was quite daunting for a beginner, but we slowly got the hang of it, and the first trick I learned was called a fakey, where you'd go up the quarter-pipe straight, then ride down backwards and spin around.

This was all happening around the time I started high school, so I was making new friends and they were all going down to the skatepark, which became our hang-out spot. There weren't many skateboarders down there; it was all about BMX and scooters.

After a few months it was obvious my bike was quickly becoming too small, but instead of looking at a new BMX, I made a detour into the scooter world. They'd become all the rage, so with a few mates we all switched over for about six months. You could obviously throw them around for tricks, but they weren't suited to practical things, like getting to the train station, so the enjoyment faded.

This corresponded with Christmas approaching, and I turned my attention to raising the funds to buy a new, bigger and better BMX. I started mowing the lawns on the weekend, which would get me twenty bucks from my parents, and by the time Santa Claus was getting ready to do his thing, I'd saved almost $300. My parents generously agreed to chip in the rest for the bike I'd chosen: a 20-inch GT Transformer. It was a thing of beauty with a white frame, blue handlebars and blue forks.

It was exciting to be back on the bike, although I soon realised it was a little bit heavy. Obviously to do tricks on a BMX the lighter the bike the better, so I again started saving my money, this time for lighter parts to upgrade my Transformer instead of getting a whole new bike. For most kids, getting twenty dollars for doing odd jobs would be gone within hours, usually spent on junk food. I'd learned from a young age to use my money wisely since my parents were forever telling me to use your money for what you want – don't waste it.

By this stage I'd lost Nathan – lost in the sense that he was no longer into BMX. He'd had a big crash that knocked his tooth out and never went back. He couldn't shake what had happened and became scared of crashing.

Getting hurt never entered my mind, even after what had happened to Nathan, and instead I went the other way, spending every spare minute down at the skatepark. My daily routine would have Mum picking me up from Marsden State High School, which was about a five-minute drive from home, at 2.45 pm. I'd race inside, change out of my school clothes, quickly have something to eat and by 3.15 pm I'd be at the skatepark, where I'd stay until it was nearly dark.

On weekends we would take the train to Beenleigh, which was only ten minutes away, to the best skatepark in the district. When you first lay eyes on Beenleigh you think you've found your skating nirvana – there are ramps, banks and walls everywhere. Big ones, small ones, tall ones – all shapes, all sizes – end to end and ongoing.

There was a really good BMX scene there, given that two of Australia's best professional riders had learned their craft at that park.

The pinnacle in BMX competition was the X Games. It was an annual extreme sports event in America organised and televised on ESPN. It was watched by millions around the world and featured the world's best BMX riders, skateboarders and motocross riders.

Colin Mackay was regarded as the first Australian rider to make a career out of BMX in the US, and he was a regular X Games competitor while Ryan Guettler followed him shortly after and won two X Games bronze medals. Both were local Beenleigh boys, which meant I literally now lived just down the road from the home of BMX in Australia.

The only way to learn new tricks was either copying someone who was better than you at the park or spending hours watching YouTube videos. The fact Mackay and Guettler had made the big time from the same town gave us all a boost. If they could do it, why couldn't we?

There was a crew of six of us – Jake, Levi, Johnno, Connor, Justin and myself – who were either hanging out at the skatepark or at each other's houses. Every weekend we'd be inseparable, riding the train line and stopping at various skateparks around Logan.

We were enthusiastic fifteen-year-olds, but we had a plan: 'If we learn a trick every day, how good are we going to be when we're twenty?'

The Under 16s competition at Logan Village Skatepark was my first career victory.

A small trophy, which I still have somewhere, was my reward for a run that consisted of some basic tricks, such as one-handers, no-footers, 360s and footjams. Soon I graduated to bigger events and bigger tricks, but to do that you had to get inventive.

Learning how to do a backflip was a key moment, and while you'd practise that now into a foam pit at an indoor facility, those things weren't available back in the day in Logan.

This is where Dad came to the rescue. He would travel around the neighbourhood collecting old mattresses that people had put out on the nature strip to be taken away as hard rubbish. While my parents didn't know a lot about BMX, they were always supportive, transporting me and my mates to competitions. But the mattress collecting was a crucial role.

Dad would bring them down to the skatepark and place them on the ramps for safety. It was easier to learn a backflip on a scooter first, because you had to get used to that feeling of being upside down. The scooter is a lot lighter, so it's easier to flip. There's also nothing in between your legs, obviously, so you can jump off to the side and land on your feet if something isn't right.

The backflip is all about commitment. Once you overcome the fear, it really isn't a hard trick.

When it came time to learn on the BMX, Dad brought down three mattresses and a wheelbarrow, which he used to move some sand from the nearby sandpit over to the ramp to help soften the landing even more.

On my fourth attempt I nailed it and actually flipped over the mattresses and landed on the grass bank. It was a significant moment because not too many people around the local area were doing backflips. Unless they had a private set-up in their backyard, which was very rare, there was nowhere to learn them.

Each new trick had a different story. The tailwhip – which is when you hold onto the handlebars and kick the bike around and then land back on it – took a long time to nail. My mate Jake Manning was further advanced than me, but he could only get one foot back down on the pedal on landing, not both.

This dragged on for six months for him, and one day after school at Crestmead I decided it was time that I really zeroed in on the tailwhips. After a couple of hours it felt like I was getting close, but we needed something more so we headed to Beenleigh the next weekend for the bigger ramp, which would give us the height we needed.

That afternoon we both landed tailwhips. It was a great moment, and I was particularly pleased given that what had taken my mate six months had taken me just one week.

Not all our learning went that smoothly.

As our thirst for new tricks and continued improvement began to rise, we started travelling to better venues and became regulars on the train to Brisbane, which was only thirty minutes away. We had access to a foam pit there, which was the safest way to learn big-time tricks, such as frontflips.

Luckily, after a couple of sessions the guys who ran RampAttak, the indoor skatepark in Brisbane, liked what they saw and generously offered free access to the facility. It was such a big help, and after a weekend of doing frontflips into the foam, I decided after school I wanted to try one at my local skatepark. I was convinced I was ready for that step, but unfortunately I wasn't. On my first attempt I didn't rotate all the way around and landed more on my back wheel, smashing up my ankle in the process. It was pretty bad, and I had to be on crutches for a couple of weeks at school.

The dynamic at school was an interesting one. Rugby League was clearly the number one sport, and they had a really good program at my high school. There were two cool groups at school, the rugby boys and the skatepark crew, and we sort of kept to our own. We didn't mess with their business, and they didn't mess with ours.

It was around this time that I became convinced my time as a student was coming to an end, and after completing Year 11 I decided Year 12 wasn't required. My mum didn't agree. She was always very strict about missing days of school and never cut me any slack on that front.

'Unless you have a job, you're going to Year 12,' she declared.

My brother had left school early; he didn't get through Year 11 as he'd lined up an apprenticeship as a painter. He did that for a year or so, but I was more keen on carpentry. After much thought, I decided to stick with school, but I'd come up with a plan. I was starting to get pretty good at BMX to the point where I was winning a lot of local competitions.

There was an event called the Core Series, which had several stops around Brisbane throughout the year. I'd started entering the pro category, rather than sticking to my age group, with the aim to accumulate as many points as possible at each event. The series winner was the one with the most points at the end of the year. There were usually about fifteen to twenty riders, with qualifying and finals on the same day. You'd do two qualifying runs then wait an hour or so and do two more in the final, with the best run counting.

The prizes for winning a stop were usually a voucher to a bike shop or parts for your bike. The grand prize at the end of the year was a cheque for $500. I won the series twice by the time I was sixteen.

While it was nice to win I didn't see that as a turning point in my career, although that did happen around that time. And it was all about a trick.

The flairwhip – a backflip with a tailwhip – was one of the biggest tricks going around. I had spent hours every night watching the professionals doing them on YouTube. My theory was that if I could learn this trick and get comfortable doing it every day, to the point where I could do it in competition, then that would put me on the same level as the pros.

It was a slow process, but I broke the trick down and focused on each part. I could do flairs, I could do backflips into the ramp, I could do backflip tailwhips over a box jump – the ingredients were all there.

When I started delivering the trick I was only sixteen, which was very young for someone to be pulling off such an elaborate trick, one that the pros were performing at the X Games. I'm not saying I was the youngest person to ever do it, but it was the trick that had people starting to take notice of my skill set.

It raised the question: what was next?

I had a decision to make, and it would be the one that would shape the rest of my life.

2

GO BIG OR GO HOME

BMX was my way out if I chose it.

I was at that crossroads moment that many teenagers face where there are two distinct pathways being presented. There was the party life and everything that came with it, and then there was a life where you didn't give in to peer pressure.

A lot of the mates who I'd started riding with had decided on the party route, as did my brother, Nathan, and I totally understood that. Don't get me wrong, I enjoyed going to parties with my mates, but there was always something gnawing away in the back of my mind.

Drugs and alcohol were prevalent from an early age, and I had my first drink at fourteen. It was easy to be seduced, particularly in a place like Logan, so that was clearly the most popular route. To understand why, you have to understand Logan.

The city is wedged between Brisbane and the Gold Coast, with a population of 350,000 living across seventy suburbs. It has been referred to as a cultural haven because of its diversity, with over 200 different nationalities living in the area. More than a quarter of the residents were born overseas. At my high school the breakdown was even more dramatic, with eighty per cent of the students coming from various backgrounds.

Unemployment and crime are the most highlighted topics when people talk about Logan City, and according to police statistics it is in the top five most dangerous places to live in Queensland.

The Logan I know isn't as bad as its reputation. In saying that, would I want to bring up my children there now? Probably not, but when I was growing up it was all I knew.

We were a typical low-income family who worked hard to make ends meet. My father, Sean, took over the family dog grooming business, Happy Hounds Dog Wash, from his dad and did that for fifteen years. I would often help him out on a Saturday to earn extra pocket money, as it was his busiest day, sometimes having up to twenty-five dogs to wash. Dad had a trailer hooked up to the back of his ute, and we'd travel all around Logan City. While I enjoyed the money I was a bit embarrassed, because I didn't think that washing dogs was a cool thing for a teenager to be doing. I was always self-conscious when we were out and about, in case someone recognised me. We always had our own dog at home, my dad's favourite breed – a Rottweiler – as well as a cat, which was usually black.

We never owned a house and instead moved around the different suburbs of Logan City, usually staying for a couple of years in each spot before settling in Crestmead. I watched first-hand what it was like to live from pay cheque to pay cheque – my mother, Donna, had a number of different jobs, including at one stage working at the local swimming pool. I always wanted a life where this struggle wasn't the way.

My parents taught me many valuable life lessons. One was to save money and not waste it. The other important thing was to have good morals and respect other people. A lot of it was the basic things, like always saying 'please' and 'thank you'. Mum was particularly big on not lying, and we would never break a promise to each other – if we pinky swore about something, then we would stick to that. This helped me realise from an early age the difference between right and wrong.

I honestly believe this respect for others that I'd learned at home was a major reason why I managed to avoid any serious trouble in my teenage years. There was a lot of violence on the streets of Logan; every Friday night you'd hear about a stabbing or an ugly brawl. There were plenty of suburbs you just had to avoid, with each cultural group having their own area or territory, so to speak. If they crossed paths, which would often happen at a party, then it was a recipe for trouble.

But if you were smart you could navigate your way through a lot of the issues.

For starters, you don't backchat the guy on the street at midnight; or if you're with a group of mates, don't yell out to the people across the street who are in a group as well.

That's the sort of scenario that ends up in a fight, and you can never rule out someone pulling a knife.

There would always be a scrap at the skateparks. You knew that some of the kids who were hanging around there were up to something they shouldn't be, rather than focusing on riding. Violence was never too far away. The other major problem was graffiti. It got to the point where the police set up a camera at Crestmead skatepark to keep an eye on what was happening. The fire brigade would also be regular visitors, given how lighting fires in the middle of the skatepark happened on a fairly regular basis.

I managed to not have too much trouble, thanks largely to my brother, Nathan, who was the opposite of me – tall and solid. I'd do my best to stand up for myself, but there was only so much I could do being a small kid, and it was soon understood that no-one really messed with me because of my big brother.

Nathan always had my back, and bullying was an issue, particularly early in my school days. I'd get bullied for the way I looked, usually because of my height, or it was often just a big kid trying to show off and I was an easy target. There was one kid in particular in my grade who kept doing it, then Nathan took care of the situation and he never touched me again.

I have no doubt that being a victim of bullying played a part in my mindset of always trying to prove that I was *better*. I raged against the notion that because I was small I couldn't do something, and those experiences clearly helped me build a strength of mind that would become invaluable down the track.

After conceding to my mother and committing to Year 12, I'd made a decision to dedicate my first year out of school entirely to BMX. That way I would find out if I was good enough to make a career out of it, and if I wasn't, well, I'd become a carpenter.

Fortunately two things happened that were in my favour. An indoor skatepark called GC Compound opened and I started hanging out with a kid from the Gold Coast named Kyle Baldock.

The new indoor facility was only a thirty-minute drive from where I lived, and it was the shot in the arm the BMX fraternity desperately needed. It created a safe training environment and a place where we could all progress our tricks, taking them to another level that was difficult to do at places like Beenleigh.

It also created a really good scene where riders from all over would come together, helping and pushing each other to be better. I quickly became a team rider for GC Compound, which meant I could have access to the facility for free at any time.

Kyle was a couple of years older than me and we clicked straightaway. He was an exceptional rider, and the beauty of our situation was that I got to feed off him, train with him every week and basically try to be like him.

He was following in the footsteps of Ryan Guettler and Colin Mackay and started making a splash on the international scene. In 2011, Kyle was the break-out star of the Dew Tour in America, the elite competition that the world's best competed in and from where you then got an invite to the X Games.

Kyle took me under his wing, and it was like a big brother–little brother sort of relationship. I looked up to him; he had a much bigger personality than I did. While I was still relatively shy, he was loud and outspoken, but we quickly formed a strong bond. Kyle always looked out for me and would vouch for me, so all I wanted to do was follow in his footsteps and listen to what advice he had.

We had first met at Beenleigh – he hadn't gone overseas at this point – and he'd posted some videos of his riding that I'd watched. We had a good time riding that day, and afterwards we both said, 'Let's do it again.' And we did almost every weekend from then on. I would catch the train there while Kyle, who didn't have his driver's licence at that stage, would get his girlfriend's mum to drive him to the skatepark.

Seeing what Kyle was achieving overseas made me have a serious think about my goals. We were best mates, we pretty much rode in a similar way, so maybe I could do this too.

Kyle was very bullish about this, and we actually got into an argument on my eighteenth birthday. He was telling me I could get to be as good as him one day, and I was telling him there was no way I could get to that level. He was yelling back at me, saying, 'Yes you will – you're that talented!'

In my opinion, I didn't have the bike control he had. I could pull out the same tricks as him, but the control wasn't there yet. I knew it would come in time, but with his continued – and often forceful – encouragement, I had a serious rethink of my goals.

There was a series in the US called the Gatorade Free Flow Tour, which was an amateur event. I'd watched a few videos about it, with the enticing part being that if you won a leg of it you went into a grand final against all the other winners for a chance to book a ticket to compete at a pro Dew Tour event.

I set my mind to going and, thanks to Kyle, I had my first-ever sponsor to help make that happen. It was a clothing company based on the Gold Coast called Sikkair who sponsored Kyle, and he convinced them to also get me involved. We promoted their clothes, which included some pretty crazy T-shirt designs, and had a Sikkair sticker on our helmets, but more importantly there was a travel budget.

They were giving me $5000 to go overseas and ride my bike, which was a dream come true, especially given I'd hardly travelled anywhere before, let alone over the other side of the world. But there was an even better carrot: the opportunity to ride at what was regarded as the epicentre of BMX freestyle – Dave Mirra's indoor warehouse in Greenville, North Carolina.

Mirra was to BMX what Michael Jordan was to basketball. He was THE man, the legend, the greatest of all time. He set a record for the most medals in BMX freestyle at the X Games (twenty-four) and won at least one medal at the event in all but one year from the competition's inception in 1995 until 2009. Fourteen of those medals were gold.

He'd built this incredible facility where the best pros would regularly get together for training blocks and, through our connection with Ryan Guettler, we'd been invited to come over and check it out.

I was travelling with another rider from GC Compound, Dale O'Brien, who was in a similar boat to me – he wanted to find out if he had what it took to make a career out of the sport. His parents had helped put the travel plans together, because as teenagers just out of school, we didn't have much of an idea what we were doing.

By this stage I'd been through a few bike upgrades. I'd had a red Colony Endeavour from a local company that had sponsored Guettler, and now I was going with the brand Sunday. This particular bike also had parts from a few different manufacturers to ensure it was as light as possible. This was a major benefit when I had to pack it up into a large travel bag for golf clubs, which was what BMX riders used when travelling on planes. You'd take the handlebars and front wheel off then stuff it all into the bag, which would go into oversized luggage.

Dale and I had certainly thrown ourselves into the deep end with this trip and – talk about being wet behind the ears – I was blown away when we got off the plane in Los Angeles and saw police walking around carrying machine guns. 'Holy hell, get a photo of this,' I said, perhaps unwisely.

We finally found our way across the country to Greenville, which was to be our base for the next two months. It was mind-blowing stuff in so many ways. I thought Logan City was rugged, but there was more violence going on in Greenville than I wanted to know about. We'd hear on the radio that someone had been shot downtown where we'd been partying the night before.

On the bike, I'd come up just short in my aim to get a slot on the Dew Tour. I did win the amateur event, which put me into the final with eleven other riders for a gig at the next

Dew Tour stop. Unfortunately, I finished second, but the experience was invaluable.

While we only got to meet Dave Mirra briefly and shake his hand, his facility was amazing, although our stay was marred by an incident that would have long-standing ramifications. (We'll explain that a bit later . . .)

But what my first overseas jaunt did was make clear that a carpentry career wasn't happening.

DONNA MARTIN

Mother

From the time he was born, Logan has always been on the go. He only has one speed, and that is just to keep going, no stopping, just keep going. He's never had any fear in his life, never. When he was young he used to call his father 'Dadin'. He couldn't say daddy or dad – it was always Dadin. And when he learned to crawl, it was only with one knee, and he'd drag the other one along. It was seriously like the Hunchback of Notre Dame – he'd get on one knee and drag the other along.

His brother is nothing like him. They are two different people – both great guys but totally different people. When his brother was younger he was very fast at running and stuff like that, so we put him into athletics, and Logan followed. Logan would do his best – his little legs would be running and going so fast – but he was always so small. He was always coming second, and we'd say, 'Don't worry about it. As long as you are having fun, just get out there and enjoy it.'

When he played Rugby League he was a little Alfie Langer. His brother was in Under 8s, and I think Logan had just started playing football. They needed somebody to fill in, and they asked if Logan could do it. He beat half of those kids that were there. It was unbelievable what he was doing – darting through their legs and everything. Everyone couldn't believe it. This little fella, smaller than everyone else, was getting the big fellas down. He has always been like that. He has always wanted better for himself – always. Even with his schoolwork, he kept pushing himself to be better.

We have always lived in Logan City, but we moved over to Crestmead, across from a school, and there was a skatepark around the corner. His brother was the one who used to go to the skatepark, and Logan thought, *I'll follow him down there.* He had such a good time. That's all he wanted to do – and that's all he did, every day after school. He actually said to me when he got into riding, 'Mum, I wish I had got into this instead of playing football.'

I never had to worry about where he was going when he was a teenager. A lot of these teenagers go out, and they do destructive things. He never did. He used to get up every Saturday morning at seven, gather all of his mates, and be like, 'C'mon we're going over here.'

They'd jump on the train with their bikes and I could trust him. I knew he would be gone all day, and I knew he would do the right thing. But it seemed like every time he would come home from the park, he would say, 'Mum, I need another tyre for the bike.' I was down at the bike shop every day. He'd have a puncture here, a puncture there, and I was like, 'What the hell are you doing down there at the park?'

Back in those days you had to stay at school. You had to finish Year Twelve, unless you had an apprenticeship or something. He got an opportunity to be an apprentice carpenter and was only there for one day. He didn't like sweeping up all the time. When he finished high school he said, 'Mum, can I have twelve months off?' I said, 'What do you mean twelve months off?' He said, 'Can't I look for a job until I see if I can make it in BMX?' I said, 'That's not a problem – you've got twelve months.' Then he said, 'The only thing is, I want to live in America for three of those months. To get anywhere, I have got to go over there.'

Logan was only seventeen, and I said, 'You're not going by yourself.' His mate Dale said he'd go with him, so off they went. He ended up winning a competition over there. He'd only been in the US eight weeks when he phoned and said, 'Mum, I need more money, can you send me over another thousand dollars?' I said, 'Okay, on one condition: when you make it big, you have to give it back to me.'

When he turned eighteen, he went out and got drunk, which is fair enough. He then said, 'I don't like how I felt the next day, and to get anywhere I have to have a clear mind, so I've got to not drink to do that.' And that's what he's done; he's phenomenal.

A lot of people say the Logan City area is pretty scummy and all that. I have lived in Logan City for thirty-two years, and I have lived in Woodridge, which is apparently the worst place, and I have never had a problem. Logan never had a problem. I think it's just the kind of person you are. If you are a bad person, well, you are going to attract bad things, but it never affected my kids. It certainly never affected Logan at all – he has just done his own thing and hasn't worried about anything else.

When I first saw him doing all the tricks, I couldn't watch – I still get anxious today. I would take him down to the skatepark in Coomera, and I would be sitting there watching, and every time he would go and do something I'd think, *I can't watch this. Oh no.* I would close my eyes; I would get anxious. He was at a competition overseas recently, and I was watching it live at one in the morning. I was getting so anxious in the stomach – *I can't watch, I can't watch.* I'm still like that after all these years.

With the Olympics, I was wiping away the tears, I was so anxious. I was actually in a daze when he won. I knew he would do it, but I didn't want to jinx it. I'm glad he did it – he went there for gold. He didn't go there for any other colour. When he was up on that podium, I wished I could have been able to be there with him. I was so amazed that all his hard work had paid off. I had a lot of people ring me up, people who I hadn't heard from for years and years. I'd ask, 'Who are you?' and they'd say, 'We went to school together back in the day.'

Logan always said he wasn't going to have kids until he was thirty, but then with his father being so ill, he thought he would start earlier if he found the right girl. He met Kim, and they hit it off straightaway. She does wonders for him, and he does wonders for her. They're good for each other. I'm so happy that he's got everything he's wanted. When he first started out riding, his aim was to get to X Games, and he got there. The next one was an Olympic gold medal, and he got that.

I never thought I would have an Olympic gold medal-list for a son – it never occurred to me – but I'm so glad he got the gold. He deserves it for all his hard work over the years. He deserves everything he gets.

3
MAKING THE CHANGE

Alcohol was out.

That was it, I was done. There wasn't a specific moment after a bender or anything like that. I'd just come to the realisation that if I wanted to make something out of BMX then sacrifices would have to be made.

Waking up every day feeling refreshed and ready to ride my bike had to be the way forward if I was going to be successful.

I'd certainly indulged in the States, where we got into a routine of going out all night, sleeping until lunchtime and then riding in the afternoon. That was fun because I was there to enjoy the experience, but it wasn't how I wanted to live my life.

Finding my first girlfriend was also a factor, given I figured I no longer had to go out to parties and get a few drinks under my belt to get up the courage to talk to girls.

My mindset was that I would do everything possible to be a success, and not drinking was something I knew I could do to help the situation. I'd been around alcohol all my life, and I didn't need to be like that. (And I was a man of my word. I didn't have another drink for five years.)

I actually didn't know what it took to be a professional athlete, and I wasn't doing any of this off the back of anyone's advice. It was just how I perceived it looked like, and as well as the alcohol going, I started eating healthier foods and began working out.

At the start it was just little things, like when we hung out at GC Compound the call was always, 'Okay, boys, let's go get Macca's.' Instead of the big yellow arches, I started getting Subway. Then, as I learned more about what was best to fuel my body, processed food got the flick. Soft drinks were quickly taken off the agenda, and the old can of Coke became a distant memory.

This new desire to become a professional was good in theory, but for some things it was a bit premature. I had to find ways to put food on the table. Fortunately, I was able to utilise my BMX skills by doing shows for a company called JC Epidemic.

It was a Christian company that would go around to schools preaching about Jesus, and they would use the BMX trick shows as a way of illustrating how it was a cool thing to be positive about God. The funny thing was, I wasn't religious in any way, but it was a good gig that Kyle Baldock had hooked me into.

The ramp we rode was on the back of a truck and, with the use of hydraulics, it would fold out into a half-pipe. It took about fifteen minutes to set up, so we'd do the show, pack up and head on to the next school.

We drove all over Australia performing shows, including a Christian music festival called Easterfest in Toowoomba. We also went to Darwin and hung out with some of the Aboriginal communities up in Katherine, where we'd do our thing and also help fix their bikes.

It was an amazing opportunity and a really rewarding experience, working with some good people. The money was certainly handy – we'd earn about $300 a day if we did two schools – although I didn't have too many expenses since I was still living at home.

But I no longer had a sponsor, thanks to Sikkair going bust when I returned from America. I'd actually planned on staying home in 2012 to work on my skills, but that changed when another of Australia's professional riders, Andy Buckworth, reached out.

He was three years older than me and had been a pro since 2008. He was originally from the Central Coast in NSW, but we'd started riding together a bit and fortunately he'd taken me under his wing.

Andy had a clothing sponsor, Jetpilot, and they were doing a 'Night of Nights Show', where all the bosses from the company would be there, so he encouraged me to come along and be a part of it. They loved what we'd done and, shortly after, I had a contract for 2012 that again included a travel budget.

The timing couldn't have been better given that out of the blue I received an invitation to an event in Paris. Now I could go, and fortunately I also got some extra spending money from an unexpected source.

The week before I left I went down to the local RSL. The previous week I'd been there with my mate Cameron, and we'd put in five dollars each and won $150 on the poker machines. This time Dad had lent me ten bucks, and I went straight back to the same machine from a week earlier. What do they say about lightning striking twice? Well, it did.

The lights started flashing and bells started ringing on the machine after just a couple of spins – I'd hit the jackpot to the tune of $1100. I couldn't believe it. I was in no way a gambler. This had just been a couple of random goes on the machines for a bit of fun. I happily reimbursed Dad his ten dollars when I got home and packed the rest away for Paris.

I was hoping to keep riding my luck when I got to the FISE (International Extreme Sports Festival) event in the French capital. It was being held on an indoor mini-ramp, which is two half-pipes sitting back to back of each other with a spine in the middle of it. There are no box jumps or transfers.

The competition format was two forty-second runs plus a best-trick component. It was an amazing atmosphere and I was excited to put together a couple of clean runs and then nailed my flair double-whip as my big trick.

I was so blown away by just being able to compete with some of the best riders in the world that when the result came through I was shocked: I'd done it. I'd won my first professional event.

In second place was Daniel Dhers from Venezuela, who was a four-time X Games gold medallist. He was the cream of the crop, and I'd just taken him down. It was the confirmation I'd been looking for that I was legitimate. I could compete at the top level.

It was a cause for celebration . . . with a bottle of water.

4

GOING PRO

1 July 2013. That was the day I became a professional BMX rider. I'd always said I wouldn't call myself one until I'd signed my first salary deal. Well, I now had three companies paying me, which well and truly fulfilled my dream of being able to make a living off the sport.

My clothing sponsor Jetpilot had renegotiated a new deal, and I'd also signed with Rockstar Energy Drink and bike brand Hyper BMX. These were both massive in the sense of having such large companies jumping on board so early in my career.

Rockstar wasn't as well known in Australia as it was in the US, but to put it in context, it was on the same level as Red Bull and Monster in terms of popularity. Hyper was also an American brand that had been more focused on the BMX racing scene but were now looking to expand into freestyle. Again, they were a big deal in the States, with their low-end bikes being massive sellers through the major department store chain Walmart.

Both clearly saw my potential, and it had all come off the back of what I'd declared was the turning point of my career.

The FISE event at Montpellier, France, in May was the most spectacular and highly regarded event on the calendar. The setting was amazing, with the course set in the gully of this huge park in the middle of the city. There were banks on either side that would be filled with more than 100,000 fans each day. It was the largest freestyle sports event in Europe, featuring BMX, skateboarding, rollerblading and moto-cross. There would be DJs pumping out music throughout all the events, and the atmosphere was insane, particularly at night.

All the best riders in the world never missed Montpellier, and it was a dream come true to be in the field, given I'd watched videos of the event heaps of times. Thankfully I didn't get too overwhelmed and finished first in qualifying, which certainly gave the confidence a boost. In the final you had a one-minute run and then a best trick component, with the combined score determining your finishing position.

I was stoked with the way I rode my run, and I'd already thought long and hard about what I was going to do in the trick segment. I'd learned to do a 1080 barspin – three full rotations while spinning the handlebars – which had never been done before. This was the time to unleash it. I was so in the moment that I wasn't thinking about where I was placed, or if I was going to win the event, or even if I should do a safer trick to make sure of my position.

This was my big chance to show the world who Logan Martin from Australia was.

I landed it on my first go.

The crowd went berserk; it was one of the most amazing things I'd ever experienced. And it kept getting better with the trick sealing the deal.

Just a few weeks earlier I'd been on the phone to an agent in America, trying to convince him to take on this nineteen-year-old from the other side of the world. His name was Lucas Mirtl, and the guys at JC Epidemic had been encouraging him to take me on.

'Do you think you can do well at competitions?' was one of Lucas's first questions.

'I know I can. I have the potential. I'm not bullshitting you,' I said.

Then I went and won Montpellier. Lucas quickly jumped on board and has been with me ever since.

My profile was building quickly, and I'd already figured out that social media was the perfect tool to promote my brand. I'd started downloading clips from practice showing off some of my big tricks on Instagram and Facebook in 2010; I figured it would be a major plus for companies to see I already had a large following.

Those numbers started to shoot up after Montpellier, and I leaned on Andy Buckworth a lot during this period. He'd been through all this and was always into me about using my money wisely, but there was more to it than just that. He told me not to promote companies for free, because I was now running a business.

His advice: *Never undersell yourself.* If a company didn't agree with what I was asking for or didn't value what I was bringing to the table, then move on. There will be better opportunities in the future.

Andy taught me how to write emails properly, with the right structure so that they looked professional when I was engaging with potential sponsors. Little things like that were so important because I needed to be as professional as I could and maximise as many opportunities as I could given sport only provides a relatively short window.

In a sport like BMX, the demands on the body are intense, the risk of injury is high. No matter how good you are, your time at the top is limited simply because the next generation is always getting better and chasing hard.

Ironically, it was an email – or lack thereof – that would haunt the next phase of my career.

I had two major goals: win an X Games gold medal and buy a house using money earned from BMX.

There is no qualifying or ranking system when it comes to the X Games. It is purely invitational, which means it's completely in the hands of the organisers as to who gets to compete on the biggest stage in BMX.

I'd started to push my name up into consideration after the victory in Montpellier, which I'd followed up with more good results at the start of 2014. People now knew who I was, and an invite finally did come . . . as an alternate.

There are only twelve riders selected from around the world, with two alternates who are there in case someone gets injured and they then slide into that slot. While I was disappointed – they were clearly sticking with some of the older, better-known riders in order to accommodate the TV audience – I sucked it up and made the trip over to Austin, Texas, for the June event.

I wanted to soak up as much as I could and get an understanding of what the whole X Games phenomenon was all about. It had been around since 1995 when sports television network ESPN realised there was a gap in the market, with Gen Xers shying away from the traditional American fare of gridiron, baseball and basketball. Extreme sports were on the rise so they acted, creating a summer competition that included events like BMX biking, skateboarding and motocross, and a winter version involving skiing, snowboarding and snowmobiling.

The first summer X Games was held in Rhode Island and attracted more than 200,000 spectators. It was hailed a major success, and from there the event has never looked back, getting bigger and better every year.

The atmosphere was insane in Austin. There were over 40,000 rowdy spectators each day, with different extreme sports happening all over the place.

The skateboarding was right next to the BMX skatepark. Up on the hill were dirt jumps for Moto X, and there was also a rally car and truck event. It was all jammed into four days of non-stop action.

Now I understood what all the hype was about!

It was epic and even better than I'd imagined. What the experience certainly did was provide a clear motivation over the next year to ensure I was part of that final twelve. Winning was a good start, and I began to have more success on the newly created FISE World Series tour, which had stops in France, Malaysia, China and Andorra.

As I told my agent, Lucas, when we were sussing each other out, I was ready to compete straightaway. I'd done all the work; I wasn't coming in with my training wheels, so to speak. I knew I was good enough to be successful.

The wins came in 2015, but the X Games email never did. Not even an alternate spot.

I was shocked.

It was definitely a slap in the face, but I knew I couldn't let it affect me too much. I could only keep doing my best at each event, keep training with the same intensity, and one day it would come.

The 2015 FISE World Series title certainly proved I'd harnessed my energies in the right way, although there was still a lot of hovering around the computer waiting for the much-anticipated X Games email in 2016.

Lucas assured me it was coming my way, but I refused to believe it until I saw it with my own eyes. Thankfully, this time he was right.

I was going back to Austin for the 2016 edition as a member of the chosen twelve, and I'd be bringing with me a sizeable chip on my shoulder. Not that I needed any more motivation, but I was certainly going there with the intention of proving to them that they should have invited me sooner.

There was a tinge of sadness around that year's edition after the shock death of Dave Mirra earlier in the year. He'd sadly taken his own life at the age of forty-one, and it was revealed afterwards that he'd suffered from CTE – the degenerative brain disease associated with concussions.

Understandably, it rocked the BMX world.

For two decades Mirra had been the face of the sport, dragging it into the mainstream and inspiring a generation of fans. He'd been on the cover of magazines, hosted a show on MTV and fronted his own video game series. He was the first rider to land a double-backflip and the first to win three gold medals at a single X Games.

I'd only met him once briefly at his warehouse. He'd finished competing by the time I arrived on the scene, so unfortunately I didn't get to share many experiences with him.

As a tribute, the X Games introduced a Best Trick contest, naming it in Dave Mirra's honour. He used to ride with gold parts, including gold pedals, so the trophy for the best trick was a gold pedal.

I'd decided not to do anything new for my debut in the big time; I just wanted to be consistent and see where that played out. I was stoked with my first run, which put me in a good headspace for the second round, which I was also happy about.

The result almost crept up on me because I was over to the side, soaking up the unbelievable atmosphere, when it registered that the final rider had gone and I was still sitting in second place.

'Did I just win a silver medal at the X Games?' I screamed.

It turned out I was the first athlete in eight years to win a silver medal at their first X Games. I also came second in the Best Trick – I did a quad-whip on the box jump – behind my mate Kyle Baldock, who produced an epic 720 double-whip.

I'd certainly guaranteed my spot for the next year, and it was also my biggest payday, given it was the norm for an energy drink sponsor to match the prize money earned at X Games, which was around $50,000 over the weekend.

The good times kept rolling as I claimed back-to-back FISE world titles after I'd held off Daniel Dhers again to win the 2016 crown. Not that anyone would know back in my home country. The media coverage was virtually non-existent; BMX in Australia was still very much a minor sport.

But away from the track changes were happening. I'd just broken up with my girlfriend of four years and moved back into my parents' place. I desperately needed a break, so I contacted my mate Jack Fahey, who was living in the States, and told him I was coming over to visit.

Jack is originally from Bundaberg in Queensland, and we'd hung out a lot in my early days. I just wanted a change of scenery and went over there for a month. Jack was returning to Australia early in 2017, and during my stay he'd started talking over social media to a girl back home.

We'd done a clip of some tricks on YouTube, and Jack told her to have a look at it. She had a friend named Kim with her, and they were both impressed with our work. Included in the feedback was a message from Jack's friend, suggesting I should make contact with Kim.

It was the message that changed my life forever.

5

TOKYO CALLING

I was just starting my practice session in Montpellier when Daniel Dhers approached. We hadn't spoken a word to each other in six years.

If we were in a room together, we wouldn't even look in each other's direction. If I was in a lift, he wouldn't get in. It was full-on and had got to the point where it was becoming obvious to the other riders that there was a serious rift between us.

It all stemmed back to my visit to Dave Mirra's warehouse in Greenville back in 2011. It was a private facility and you only got in there if you knew someone or were considered good enough to hang out with the crew.

Fellow Aussie Ryan Guettler had got me over there, and midway through the stay, he and some of the other professional riders had to go away for two weeks of competitions. I'd already competed in an amateur event, so I was just hanging around the warehouse, practising every day.

'Here's the key,' Guettler said. 'Keep coming to do your sessions, but make sure you lock it up. Don't be a disgrace in the place, be respectful, and whatever you do don't tell Daniel Dhers I gave you the key.'

Mirra wasn't there – he'd popped his head in briefly and then left – so Dhers was effectively the manager of the place. He'd gone off to compete with Guettler, so basically my mate Dale and I had the run of the place. Then a few of the younger guys, including British rider Ryan Taylor, came back early from the trip, so we had a group of five riding the warehouse every day.

We knew when Dhers was expected back, so we had one last session the day before. The problem was, Taylor and his mate left their bikes locked inside the warehouse.

Dhers arrived back and immediately went on a witch-hunt to find out how the bikes got there. He rang Ryan straight-away, because he was the only other person who had a key. After a heated discussion, Ryan denied giving anyone the key and then rang me immediately.

'Daniel is going to call you. Do not tell him I gave you the key, because it's going to mess me around,' Ryan said.

I completely freaked out. I was there just living out a dream, and now I found myself in what was quickly becoming a major international incident. I'd idolised these guys, watched hundreds of clips of Dhers, and in particular Mirra, who was the first guy to really explode the sport. I used to watch them and think, *Far out, I want to do what they're doing.*

The phone ringing shook me out of my stroll down memory lane. As expected, it was Dhers calling.

'Have you been having any sessions while we were away?' he asked. 'I'm not accusing you, but you're one of the guys that is still here, and I'm going to call everyone who stayed back.'

I couldn't stitch up Ryan, who had been so good to me, so I had to lie. 'I didn't have the key,' I said.

Dhers called a meeting at the warehouse later that afternoon for all the riders who were in Greenville. There were ten of us in attendance, but no-one was sweating bullets more than me.

'One of you had the key,' Dhers said as he scanned the group. 'There are bikes here. Who was it?'

Everyone was staring down, avoiding eye contact. It was deathly quiet. I couldn't stand it anymore, so I fessed up. 'Yeah, it was me.'

Dhers was seriously pissed, but I was leaving anyway, so nothing much happened then. I did hear later that he and Ryan had a massive blue and were even going to come to blows about it all before they sorted it out.

Dave Mirra was also apparently furious. The way he saw it, this seventeen-year-old kid from Australia had basically trespassed in his private warehouse.

I'd tried to apologise to Dhers the following year when we crossed paths in Paris at the FISE event, which was my first professional victory. Much to my amusement he'd finished second, but he still wasn't seeing the funny side about the key blow-up.

'Hey, Daniel, I'm sorry for what happened last year,' I said.

But he shrugged it off and was almost dismissive. He didn't want a bar of what I was trying to say, so I just figured that was how it was going to be. I wasn't going to play into his game and give him the time of day if he wasn't giving me the time of day. From then on I didn't let it bother me, and clearly he wasn't letting it bother him, so we each went our own way.

Also, I was still a very shy kid at this stage, so I retreated back into my shell, and it would be years before we'd speak again.

Our beef had started to become obvious because I was appearing more and more on the podium as we traded finishing first and second at numerous FISE events, so there were plenty of opportunities for awkward moments.

That's why when Dhers offered an olive branch in Montpellier, I was pleasantly surprised.

'Hey, Logan, do you mind coming and having a chat?' he said.

I was blown away. I stopped my practice session and went over to the side of the course for an audience with my arch rival.

'Let's just cool it,' Dhers said. 'Let's just clear the air. You're going to be in the sport for a lot longer than I am. You're doing awesome, you're doing so well, and I hate that there is this tension between us.'

I was momentarily speechless before offering, 'Look, I'm sorry for what happened back then, but it is what it is. I'm more than happy to clear the air.'

I'd heard the whispers but didn't want to get too caught up in the prospect of BMX freestyle becoming an Olympic sport.

Obviously that would be incredible and open up all sorts of possibilities, but right now my immediate challenge in 2017 was to chase my first X Games gold medal.

That's what I was focused on as I arrived in Croatia in June for a key lead-up event, the Pannonian Challenge. However, that all changed when I was approached by Richard King, a British guy who was involved in the running of the X Games and other major BMX events around the world.

He had this excited look on his face – and with good reason. 'We're in,' he said.

According to King, the UCI (Union Cycliste Internationale), the world governing body for sports cycling, was about to announce that BMX freestyle would be included in the 2020 Tokyo Olympic Games.

Even though there had been rumours, the confirmation still caught me by surprise. It was crazy because I was just getting to my prime now, and I'd only be twenty-six by the time Tokyo came around.

Straightaway I started mapping out in my head a plan to ensure that I would still be at my peak in three years' time.

There had been a push to include more extreme sports in the Olympics as they looked to engage the younger generation. BMX racing had been in since 2008, and skateboarding had got approval for Tokyo twelve months earlier.

In a way it was weird because BMX has always been such an individual sport. We didn't have coaches. We hung out and trained with each other, and travelled around together from competition to competition, but we were still doing our own thing.

Would that change now that our sport had been given the Olympic thumbs-up? There were so many questions about what it all meant, but the general consensus was that the world of BMX freestyle was about to change forever.

In a way, I was already a poster boy for change.

The professionalism I'd brought to the tour was starting to rub off on some of my competitors. My ethos of no drinking and no partying had made me the odd one out from the start. No-one could understand initially what I was doing, because the perception had always been that life as a professional BMX rider was one big party.

And it wasn't far from the truth.

Each stop on the global circuit would follow a similar pattern. Party on Friday night, party on Saturday night, and then an after-party on Sunday night. This meant the lead-up to most competitions for the riders would involve going hard all night, waking up with a hangover, staying in bed until lunchtime before shaking themselves off for qualifying or the final later in the afternoon.

Often there would be music festivals running alongside the extreme sports events, so there was always a lot going on in the party space, with plenty of drugs and girls available. That was just the scene, but it wasn't my scene.

At the start the guys would get into me, almost harassing me to stay out, but they soon learned it wasn't even worth asking, because they knew that wasn't my thing.

There were plenty of awkward moments because of my focused approach, especially when we had to share rooms at some events. One morning I'd got up at 6 am and was starting to cook eggs when my roommate arrived home from the night before. The contest was later that day. I ended up cooking him breakfast as well, which we ate together before he headed to bed and I started my preparation for the competition.

Even after events that I'd won I never went out to celebrate, preferring to head back to my hotel room, pack up my bike and fly out the next morning. In recent times I had noticed a change in attitude from some of my competitors. They were seeing that my results were justifying the sacrifices of not drinking and being vigilant about fitness and diet.

And there were more email invites coming too.

This time around there was an added extra in the X Games correspondence. Clearly I was starting to make my mark, as I was now considered good enough to take part in *two* of the BMX freestyle disciplines – there were six overall – at the event.

The park was my specialty, but there was also a dirt category. This event was held on a course where the jumps were made out of compacted soil, and they were all in a straight line. Every feature was so much bigger – steeper drop-ins, higher take-offs, bigger down ramps and bigger air time.

It was a completely different discipline, and the main reason I hadn't competed much in dirt was the lack of opportunities to do so in Australia. There weren't a lot of courses around when I was coming through the ranks, but I'd learned to adapt my jumps to make it work, and I was more than happy to do so on the sport's biggest stage.

Every three years the X Games moves location, and 2017 was the first year in Minneapolis, where it was held in the

U.S. Bank Stadium, a spectacular indoor venue that had opened the year before and was the home of the NFL's Minnesota Vikings.

One word summed up my second X Games: silver.

I backed up my silver medal in the park event from the previous year with a silver in the dirt behind a young American kid, Colton Walker. And then in the Best Trick competition, I claimed my third silver medal behind my good mate Kyle Baldock.

While the gold had eluded me again, I still found myself able to enjoy what had gone down in Minneapolis. The reason? I now had someone to celebrate with.

This chick is super cool and super easy to talk to.

That's what was going through my head from the first couple of long-distance conversations I had with Kimberley Berroya, the girl I'd been introduced to through Jack Fahey's friend. We'd hit it off straightaway, and that continued when we first met on the Gold Coast after I returned from America in February. By May we were dating and then, when I bought my first house in September, Kim moved in.

She was a gymnastics teacher and had been an elite junior in the sport, which in many ways is an interesting link. Often when I'm asked to describe freestyle BMX, I say it's gymnastics on a bike, with all the spinning and flipping across different elements.

Kim had grown up in Ulladulla on the NSW coast and at the age of eleven was accepted into the Australian Institute of Sport for gymnastics. She'd actually gone along to support a friend who was trying out for a spot and ended up getting picked.

She moved to Canberra, where the AIS is based, with her mother and younger brother to train with a squad of the best gymnasts in Australia. She only lasted three months, as it quickly became obvious that the strict and overbearing lifestyle wasn't for her.

Kim continued competing at state championship level until she was sixteen, but now she was making a living out of gymnastics as a coach. In many ways it helped our relationship, because she had an understanding of the mindset and preparation required to pursue a demanding career in sport.

Although, I did wear her patience a bit thin in the early days of our relationship before she got used to my structured lifestyle.

Before we lived together, I would stay over at her house but leave at 6 am because I had to get ready to go riding at 9 am. She wasn't particularly impressed with that, nor the fact I was also an early-to-bed person, sometimes even by 8 pm. The routine was all a part of the sacrifices that were a major part of my life, and Kim came to understand my quirks.

The best thing was she understood *me*, and from the jump she was fully supportive of my quest to be the best in the world.

And I was going to get the chance to be just that, literally.

The Tokyo Olympics announcement had already resulted in significant changes to my sport, the most notable being the creation of a BMX freestyle world title under the banner of the 2017 UCI Urban Cycling World Championships.

I quite fancied the idea of being the first ever world champion.

The championships were held in November in Chengdu, China, and it was a whole new world for us. We travelled as a team under the banner of Cycling Australia, who had come on board since the Olympic announcement. They'd been awesome to deal with because they didn't force themselves on us, so to speak. They explained how they were new to BMX freestyle and weren't there to rock the boat.

From their perspective, it was all about supporting us in any way they could, which was music to my ears.

Part of that would be providing funding for events like the world titles, where for the first time I'd be wearing an Australian insignia on my T-shirt, which was pretty cool. There was another promising rider wearing the green and gold: Sydney's Brandon Loupos was also proving himself to be a serious player on the world scene.

But before we got the opportunity to ride for our country, there was some other business to take care of. The final event of the FISE World Series was a week before the world championships, and it was also in Chengdu but at a different skatepark.

It proved to be a thrilling final after the series leader, Daniel Dhers, failed to get out of the semifinals. This meant the scenario in the final was simple for me – finish first and I win my third consecutive FISE World Series crown; come second and Dhers wins the overall title.

Despite being very happy with my runs and coming up with a best score of 92.20, it wasn't enough, with American Nick Bruce just pipping me with a 92.60. I quickly computed that result and spun it into a positive: I would get to ride again a week later for an even bigger prize.

The world championships went exactly to script as I finished on top of the rankings through the qualifying round and the semifinals, with my teammate Brandon Loupos in second place. This form continued into the final, where I produced two consistently high standard runs, which was rewarded with an average score of 93.82.

It was enough to push Britain's Alex Coleborn down to second – Loupos faded for tenth place – which meant the Australian flag was flying at the top of the pole in the inaugural world championships.

Given I loved winning so much, I was pumped with the result, but I wasn't ready for the emotions that hit afterwards. I hadn't fully appreciated coming in to the event how significant it was, given how the X Games had always been placed on a pedestal.

There is a tradition in professional cycling where world champions are presented with a rainbow jersey, which they then wear during races for the next twelve months. It's mainly white with five horizontal bands in the UCI colours around the chest. From the bottom up the colours are: green, yellow, black, red and blue, the same colours that appear in the rings on the Olympic flag.

I was now the proud owner of the first ever BMX freestyle rainbow jersey.

Being Australia's first world champion struck something deep in me, and I realised how much I'd wanted to win it. I was clearly still riding a wave of emotion when I arrived back home; I did something that I hadn't done for five years.

I had a drink.

Kim and I had arranged to go on a cruise, and she enjoys having the odd cocktail, so I did the same. I'd also had McDonald's for the first time in years a couple of days before the cruise, so clearly I was in celebration mode.

It was a pivotal moment because my personal life and professional life had come together in perfect unison. I was happy, I was world champion, and I wanted to enjoy it.

6

CRASH, BURN, RISE, REPEAT

There is a comfort in getting uncomfortable.

Every day I'm riding on an adrenalin rush and constantly scaring myself – some days more than others, particularly if I'm trying new things or almost crashing. That's why there's a sense of pride walking away from each session, because you've overcome the fear.

The positive endorphins running through your body give you a feeling that is so addictive. You *crave* it. And that rush comes about only because you've pushed yourself out of your comfort zone.

And you've survived.

The ability to overcome fear has a lot to do with your personality; it's like you're constantly having an internal chat with yourself. If I do crash my mindset isn't, *What if I get hurt again?* Straightaway I'm thinking, *When can I get back into it?*

I'm aware of the risks. I know what can go wrong, but I prefer to look at it in a positive light: what can go *right*. That is a better way to look at life and the precarious situations that I'm constantly confronted with in BMX.

People often ask what I'm thinking about during tricks. Because I've been doing this for seventeen years – professionally for nine years – I'm a lot more conscious of what's going on in the trick or in a spin. As soon as I take off from the ramp I can feel if something is about to go wrong, or I can feel if something is about to go right.

I know how to control things to a point. If I need to I can correct it in the air, or if I'm going to crash, I can slide out a little bit more smoothly than I would have ten years ago, because I have more awareness of where I am and how the trick has gone wrong.

When I first learned backflips I would shut my eyes in the middle of the trick, only opening them to see the landing. That was because I was scared to do the trick for a long time but, like a lot of things, the more you do them the more comfortable you become. I've found that the more relaxed you are on the bike, the more in control you are of what is happening around you.

But sometimes it doesn't work out that way.

My first competition of 2018 was a small dirt contest over in America at a Supercross event. I lost my bearings on a jump and paid a hefty price, landing face-first on the ramp, which I then slid all the way down. It was a solid crash but I came away relatively unscathed – just a bit of whiplash.

Unfortunately, it was a sign of things to come.

When I got home my focus turned to the opening FISE World Series event of the season, which was in a new location: Hiroshima, Japan. I'd been focusing on a couple of new tricks, including a frontflip flair, which had a high degree of difficulty. It involved a frontflip with a 180-degree rotation, landing back on the ramp that you'd taken off from.

On this particular day we were in Brisbane at the indoor skatepark RampAttak, and Kim had tagged along. She would often take video of my practice sessions, which I would then post onto social media. There was one rule that I was always reminding her of: if I crashed she was to keep filming and not get scared. I wanted my followers to experience all the ups and downs of my journey.

The frontflip flair has quite a unique spin, and if you miss what we call 'the pop' it's hard to speed up the rotation. I missed the pop, got stuck upside down in the frontflip and then landed upside down, mashing my collarbone.

It was nasty.

An ambulance was called and the paramedics quickly put me on the green whistle. This is an inhaler with special medication in it that provides rapid pain relief. I had initially been in extreme pain, so the whistle managed to at least make me comfortable for my trip to hospital.

Kim was understandably upset but proud that she did her job.

'I kept filming,' she said in an attempt to brighten my spirits.

Once I got to the hospital they took X-rays, which showed a broken collarbone and bruising in the lungs. I was sent home that night, where I started to do my calculations around whether I could recover for the trip to Japan in three weeks' time.

The only way to accelerate the process was to have surgery, to the tune of $10,000. I had to wait a week for the procedure, which meant I had a two-week recovery period. When I'm in a moment like this, all I can see is my goal – in this case, it was boarding a plane to Japan.

I waited until Sunday – the day before I would have to fly out – to test out the shoulder. I took the bandages off, got back on the bike and actually felt okay. However, the reality was I hadn't done anything for three weeks. My muscles weren't ready to go, and it was too much of a risk on my body.

This was the second time I'd broken my collarbone, and while my injury list was long, I felt pretty lucky compared to some of my mates. Considering how long I'd been doing this and what I'd achieved, I'd managed to escape any serious injuries that kept me off the bike for long amounts of time. By comparison, plenty of my mates are broken.

I've dislocated my shoulder six times.

The first time I did it I went to hospital and they popped it back in, but after that I learned to do it myself with the help of my mates. One time we were in France and I injured it at a contest on the Sunday, but with the help of Kyle Baldock, we popped it straight back in. I had another event in France the following weekend, so I stayed off the bike until Thursday – and then went out and won the competition.

I suffered a really bad concussion in 2017 at the Nitro World Games in Salt Lake City, Utah. I had just dropped in for my last practice run before the qualifying round, which was only twenty minutes away. I attempted a frontflip barspin no-hander. It went horribly wrong, and I ended up knocking myself out. I don't remember doing the trick, and barely remember anything from the day itself.

I continued to throw up the next day and then travelled home, still very sick. I had a headache for a week. That was certainly a scary one, but it wasn't my personality to dwell on such things or think about the potential larger consequences.

I've also torn ligaments in both of my ankles. I've dislocated one pinky finger and busted off the nails on both of them, as well as breaking a bone in my hand. I have a bulging disc in my back, the bottom line being my body never actually feels good. That's just something you get used to.

But I'm the lucky one.

There are so many stories about elite riders who have had their careers cut down because of nasty injuries. When I was coming through the ranks, one of the riders I looked up to was American Brett Banasiewicz. He was a couple of years younger than me but had broken through early in his career, winning a Dew Tour event at the age of seventeen. I idolised him because he made every trick seem easy – he looked so comfortable. All I wanted to do was look like he did on a bike.

But he had a bad crash not long after his first major win and wasn't able to get back to that elite level again. He'd suffered a brain injury, and we never got to compete against each other.

Thankfully Brett has been able to get on with his life and is still very much involved in the sport, but his story is a reminder to all of us of what could be around the corner.

*

It's my turn.

That was the vibe I was feeling when I arrived in Minneapolis for the 2018 X Games. The double silver the year before showed that I was ready, and from the moment I hit practice I just felt on with the course. Some courses suit you better than others, and this one seemed to play to my strengths.

This event was being held in a bowl, which meant a change of approach was required – a regulation FISE freestyle park was more expansive and covered an area of 1500 square metres. Generally I didn't do a lot of bowl contests because I would be scored down for doing so many tricks. Judges in bowl contests prefer smoother, higher and more flowing runs rather than the big tricks, which is my strength.

The X Games had previously been a park competition, but in recent times they'd gravitated towards the bowl. Thankfully the judges treated it as a combined event, so you weren't scored down for big tricks but you just had to make sure there was some serious big air involved.

Fortunately, I found a good line early in practice where I figured I could bring all my bigger tricks from a FISE event to this bowl contest. That's often hard to do, but I managed to link everything together, and with each day of practice I became more and more comfortable.

I'd bounced back from my injury with a second place at the FISE event in Montpellier, so there were no lingering issues. And I was determined not to be the bridesmaid any longer.

Everything went according to plan throughout the week, and the final came down to a shoot-out between myself and the 2016 champion, American Dennis Enarson.

I was stoked with the runs I'd put together, scoring a 92.66 followed up by a 93.33. But Enarson was the last rider, so I faced a nervous wait. As I looked on, I almost convinced myself that he was going to go ahead of me.

He looked pretty good, and I sensed it was his best for the competition . . . but *how* good?

91.00.

I'd done it. *I'd finally done it.*

All my life I'd dreamt of this moment. Ever since I got my first BMX at the age of twelve, the goal had been to win an X Games gold medal. And now here it was around my neck. Having Kim alongside me as I ticked off my biggest career goal made it even sweeter.

Another silver in the dirt competition and in the Best Trick saw a new dream form in my mind. *Next year, I want two X Games gold medals.*

Among the many messages of congratulations was one from Wade Bootes, Cycling Australia's BMX high-performance director and the man who was bringing the freestylers under his wing.

He was a former elite BMX racer who'd also won a mountain bike world championship during his decorated career. Having his knowledge and experience helped so much with the transition over to the 'team' vibe, given we were all so used to doing our own thing.

One of the major benefits came on the health and fitness side, where we now had access to a host of experts and various facilities around the country. Throughout my career I'd always worked out, but I'd never followed an expert's guide or anything – I just went hard at the gym because I figured it was good for me.

In 2014, I'd started working out at a gym called Fitstop in Redland Bay after my sponsor at the time, Jetpilot, had promoted a six-week challenge there. I really enjoyed the gym – it had everything I needed, including cardio classes, and even though it was a forty-five-minute drive from where I lived in Logan, I convinced myself it was a crucial part of becoming a professional.

I soon became mates with the owner, Peter Hull, and began helping him out with promotion as he started to expand the business. In many ways I was my own worst enemy in the gym, because I enjoyed pushing myself to the edge and using the workouts as a way of testing my mental strength. Fitstop provided a forty-five-minute high-intensity group workout, and each session was pre-planned, including three different types of workouts focusing on weights and cardio. I really enjoyed this system because I didn't have to create my own routines, and training in the group environment also provided this unspoken friendly competition to outwork everyone and 'win' the session.

The harder I went, the better it was for me, at least in my mind. It was providing that extra one per cent over my rivals, which I was always searching for, and fitness had been such a major part of my rise through the ranks. I'd see some of my competitors get to the thirty-second mark of their runs and noticeably run out of steam after a couple of their big tricks. They'd then struggle over the last thirty seconds because they were physically spent.

I never wanted to be like that.

However, my bull-at-a-gate attitude to the gym was starting to have some unfortunate consequences. With the bulging disc in my back, which was an understandable ailment given all the time spent leaning over the bike, it was becoming clear my workout practices weren't helping.

Enter Eric Haakonssen.

He was Wade Boote's right-hand man, the senior physiologist for Cycling Australia who took over the structure of my gym sessions. One of the first things my new strength and conditioning coach did was get me in for some extensive fitness testing, which involved being hooked up to a number of different monitors. Eric's theory was that he would focus on what would benefit me on the bike, rather than just smashing it in the gym.

Everything was geared towards two years' time in Tokyo, although getting there wasn't going to be as easy as we thought, given the complicated qualification pathway.

Only nine riders would be competing, with one of those spots already going to Japan as the host country. Riders would earn points for their countries at UCI-sanctioned events, such as the FISE World Cup stops during the qualifying period that ran from 1 November 2018 to 11 May 2020.

The country that scored the most points could send two riders, second to fifth would send one rider each, while the final two spots would go to countries based on individual rider performance at the 2019 World Championships.

It was hard to get your head around, but we were one of the few countries who had an opportunity to win two spots, given Brandon Loupos and I were clearly in the top handful of riders in the world.

Although I didn't exactly perform like that when the X Games made its debut in Australia, which is something I'm still angry about. In a massive boost for extreme sports in this country, the ESPN extravaganza came to Sydney, but unfortunately the weather in October didn't play its part.

It was a dirt event held at Spotless Stadium (now the Sydney Showground Stadium) in the Olympic Park precinct. Rain and dirt aren't a good mix, and the whole lead-up was a washout, which meant we barely got half an hour of practice on the course.

The organisers had spent a lot of time trying to harden up the jumps, even putting plywood on the floor where there were puddles in between features. It was a mess, and I struggled with the softness of the jumps, which made it hard to get enough speed coming off them.

There were three jumps, and I managed to get through the first two tricks. But with the last jump, where I was trying to do a 720 double-barspin – which is a trick I do quite often – I was coming up a bit short each time.

I was getting more and more frustrated. I kept repeating the same thing – coming up short and crashing. In hindsight, I should have dialled back the trick a little bit to make it clean, and if I'd done that I probably would have won.

The winner, Polish rider Dawid Godziek, had done a simple trick on his second jump to ensure he got over the third jump, which was a sound plan. I ended up finishing ninth and was pissed afterwards.

It had been a golden opportunity . . . and I'd blown it. But we didn't have long to stew on it; I was scheduled to defend my world title the following month back in China.

As part of the team's preparation, Wade asked us if we wanted a change of scenery from the Gold Coast for a training camp, and it was decided a few days down in Melbourne would work wonders.

There was a good indoor skatepark called RampFest, and for our sessions we set up a large airbag to soften the landing as we practised some of our bigger tricks. I decided to focus on doing a flip double-whip, which I hadn't really got the chance to do too often at home because we didn't have the same quality facility.

On the second day I went back in the morning and practised the trick again. After a couple of good run-throughs I decided to move over to the resi (a foam and plastic safety layer), where the landing wasn't as soft. I also nailed that, so I kept working my way through the rest of the session, combining various other tricks.

Then, half an hour later, I thought I should go back and do one last flip double-whip, just to confirm in my mind that I was on top of it.

It turns out I wasn't.

While I was in the air, my foot hit the wheel as the whip was coming around, which put everything out of control. Then I got my foot stuck in the top of the wheel, which meant when I landed my ankle was effectively pulled apart. The moment I hit the ground I knew I was in serious trouble. As I sat on the ground and started to take my ankle brace off,

Kyle and Loupos came over to survey the damage.

'Surely it's not that bad. I bet you wake up tomorrow and it'll be all good,' Loupos said.

'Nah, I'm telling you, it's seriously messed up.'

We went straight to hospital for X-rays, and while I waited I booked a flight home later in the day. I wanted to get as far away from this place as soon as possible. While the initial report at the hospital was positive, I still couldn't move my ankle, so I had an MRI scan on the Gold Coast. That scan revealed some spiral fractures in the high ankle, a section known as the syndesmosis, plus there was some ligament damage.

It wasn't the first time I'd rolled my ankle, and previously I'd taken painkillers, put tape around the ankle really tightly and continued riding. Not this time.

The world championships were only a couple of weeks away, but my doctor wasn't entertaining a quick recovery.

'If you make these spiral fractures worse, it's going to be a lifelong injury. It will become an issue all the time,' he said.

That wasn't what I wanted to hear, but it was apparent I was going to have to take this one on the chin and sit it out.

I'd managed to bookend the year with bad injuries. Thankfully, in between those tough times, I'd also won my first X Games gold medal.

And there was one other good thing to take out of 2018 . . . I was going to be a father.

7

BUILDING A DREAM

'We need to find a big enough property to build a skatepark or we're going to have to move overseas.'

The reality of my situation was starting to hit home as my new fiancée, Kim – we'd got engaged on New Year's Eve – and I started to think about the next phase of our lives.

Proposing had been one of the more nerve-racking things I'd ever done. We'd travelled up to Townsville in Far North Queensland to visit Kim's parents over Christmas, where we revealed to them that we were expecting a little boy. On the way home we made a detour to Airlie Beach, and we decided on New Year's Eve to get up early and watch the sunrise on the sand. I'd hardly slept the night before, constantly going over what I was going to say. I wasn't worried about her saying no; my anxiety had more to do with how I delivered the proposal.

The setting was perfect, but my delivery wasn't. I stumbled through my words, although I did have the ring to carry me.

When I got down on one knee Kim wasn't worried about my performance – thankfully, she just wanted to say yes.

Building my own skatepark was a big commitment, but for a while there had been something nagging at the back of my mind about my riding. I was still winning and competing well, but my skills weren't progressing. I'd learned enough tricks to be in the top echelon and was really just concentrating on being consistent in my execution of them.

That wasn't going to cut it for much longer. I had to find a way to go to another level over the next eighteen months leading into the Olympic Games.

The problem was the GC Compound had closed in 2015. Since the only indoor facility in the area had shut down, I had to go old school to practise my tricks, travelling around to all the local skateparks during the day while the kids were still at school.

It wasn't sustainable for a number of reasons, mainly around safety, given the ramps were clearly not the highest quality. It's always hit or miss with concrete ramps, whether they're going to be good or not. Often they have a bumpy transition, which means you can't get as much height out of it. There is also the debris factor – often smashed glass from people drinking in the park the night before, and leaves can also be a major issue. They have to be swept away because it can get very slippery.

Wooden ramps are clearly better and safer, which was what I was now contemplating in my own skatepark. The situation had evolved to the point where I now had no alternative but to build it.

I'd bought my first house in 2017 on the Gold Coast, fulfilling my childhood dream of purchasing a home off my earnings from BMX.

There were large properties out the back of Logan where my mum lived, but we didn't really want to be that far away from the coast. Then it was suggested I check out the Gold Coast Hinterland. I'd never been up that way, but the area certainly had the large land blocks that we could work with.

But finding the perfect spot was proving difficult. In some places the land was perfect but the house was no good, or vice versa. One day I was driving around Maudsland, where I'd been recommended a property, but it wasn't quite right either. However, there was another one just down the road, although I was pretty sure the land was too sloped and would be hard to work with.

I decided to go in for a look anyway, and I instantly fell in love with the house. Then, when I was standing in the backyard, I realised there was enough room to make a skatepark work because there was a large flat area before it sloped down again to the garden bed.

That afternoon I made an offer.

I already had a guy lined up to build the park. Jason Watts and I had competed against each other when we were younger in the Core Series around Brisbane. We were always battling it out for first and second, and he'd also become a professional BMX rider, but, importantly, he'd also completed a carpentry apprenticeship. He'd recently rebuilt a skatepark down in Melbourne, so I went down there to check it out and have a ride.

Jason and I got chatting about my idea and what it would cost compared to the budget I had, which was $90,000.

'We'll make it work, let's do it,' Jason said.

We bought the house in December and it took us a few months to get everything in order. There were moments in the planning process where we weren't sure if it was going to work, and the pin was nearly pulled a couple of times. The neighbours hadn't been overly impressed when I revealed my plans. Technically, I didn't have to do anything, because I didn't require a permit to build the park. It wasn't classified as a permanent structure, so it fell into the same category as playground equipment, like putting up a trampoline in the backyard.

Just before we were scheduled to start digging, I put a note in the mailbox of my surrounding neighbours to explain what I was doing. I included my contact number, so if there were any issues they should give me a call or come and knock on my door. I didn't hear anything for a week, so I thought everything was sweet . . . until I saw the lady across the street pacing up and down her driveway, taking photos of what was happening in my yard. I went over to talk to her and she fully cracked it at me. The good thing was I remained calm, which seemed to infuriate her even more before she stormed inside.

A couple of days later another neighbour from across the street came over and said the guy who lived next door was trying to get people in the street to sign a petition to stop the construction of my skatepark. I went over and knocked on their door but again didn't receive a warm reception.

What I *did* receive was a note in the letterbox from the upset neighbour with a long list of concerns, which included questioning whether there would be people urinating in the yard or using my toilet, the potential number of cars parking in the street and the noise the skatepark would generate. These concerns had also been sent to the council.

Their next move was calling a community meeting down the road at the park near the entrance to the estate. They were trying to say it was just a general catch-up with the local councillor, but I knew it was all about me and my skatepark, so I called their bluff and went down to the meeting. There was some strong debate, and I invited the councillor to come up and see what all the fuss was about. He said he'd send out a council building inspector to have a look in the coming weeks.

I was away at a competition the first time the inspector had come around, and I'd told Kim not to let anyone on the property unless I was there. She'd been impressed with the guy from the council and had said I'd call him when I returned. I did that, and Kim was right – he was very reasonable about the whole thing. There was only one minor issue regarding the maximum height of the structure being three metres from the natural ground level, but in one area we'd dug into the ground.

A month later I got a letter in the mail saying everything had been approved regarding the construction of my skatepark.

It was a crazy time in more ways than one, with Kim going into labour during the construction. On 13 May we welcomed a beautiful baby boy into the world, who we called Noah.

Coming up with baby names had certainly brought up my own unique situation, which many people found amusing. I was Logan from Logan. When I was born back on 22 November 1993, Mum and Dad didn't know what to call me, so they figured because we were in Logan Hospital in Logan then that name would do.

Fittingly, while I was getting my head around becoming a father – which was the single greatest day of my life – I got introduced to my new BMX baby. The first ride on my backyard skatepark, which would become known as Logan Land, happened while Kim and Noah were still in the hospital.

Both things were amazing and life-changing.

It was a new frontier on a number of levels.

Travelling to the other side of the world with a three-month-old baby added a layer to the preparation phase for the 2019 X Games that I'd obviously never experienced. Kim was very understanding in terms of what was required, and at night we were in separate rooms because she knew sleep was one of the most important factors for competing at an optimum level.

Being able to hang out with them throughout the week when I wasn't practising was so good. There is always a lot of downtime at major competitions, and now I had the best thing possible to keep me distracted: playing with my son.

Noah and Kim were by my side as we entered what was quickly becoming my favourite arena – U.S. Bank Stadium in Minneapolis. As usual, the atmosphere was electric on finals day, which was held on the Saturday, and I had a busy schedule with the park event in the morning followed by the dirt competition four hours later.

There were several new challenges this time around, the first being to end the streak of nine different riders winning the last nine gold medals. It was being called the 'park curse', and it certainly added intrigue to the competition, which was operating according to a very different format this year.

Twelve riders started and initially fought it out to make the top six and advance into what was called a 'super final'. And this was where things got interesting. Instead of having your best one-minute run out of two or three attempts deciding the placings, the super final format was four thirty-second runs – and they all counted.

I'd done my research and analysed the pre-competition guidelines, which the judges always released. These often gave good insights into what the judging panel were looking for at each event, because it can vary. Generally they liked big tricks, big air, going fast and landing smooth. You do all those things well and that's going to win your run. Sometimes you can pick up on what the judges are focusing on during the competition. For example, they may zero in on smooth landings, so a complete run without any bobbles might score higher than usual. If you can tune into these things during the rounds, you can adjust accordingly for the final.

It was obvious that in the changed X Games format they were seeking four completely different runs with different techniques and different lines in each of those runs. We had four days of practice in the lead-up, where I figured out which tricks and lines worked together. Then in each session I replicated the four thirty-second runs I would do in the final. Diversity was the key to my plan, and I noticed early that a number of the other riders weren't going into the same level of detail – they were mixing up their tricks but often keeping the same lines.

It was a fast-paced, intense competition, with riders dropping in just seconds after the others had finished their run. This non-stop action was all about what worked best for TV, which was what the X Games was all about.

My tactics were paying off early with seventeen-year-old Rim Nakamura, who was making his X Games debut, emerging as my main threat. He'd also seemed to have figured out that the secret to success was to do four completely different runs, although his lines appeared to be similar on a couple of them.

The crowd was certainly behind the new kid on the block, and he nailed his final run, which made me slightly nervous. I knew I just had to execute a nice, clean run to maintain my lead, which I thought I'd done, but the wait for the result was excruciating. It felt like five minutes – it was probably less than one – before the result flashed up on the big screen.

I'd done it. I'd broken the curse. Back-to-back gold.

There was no official medal ceremony at the X Games. The moment the result flashed up on the screen an official was in front of you, the gold medal was around your neck and there was a camera in your face.

As I was biting the medal for the standard winning-photo pose, Kim and Noah joined me for a touching moment, although my son appeared to be sleeping through all the excitement, which was a good thing!

I could actually relate to how Noah was feeling a few hours later when it was time to start the thirty-minute warm-up for the dirt final. I was seriously tired. The hectic nature of the park event, combined with the heat inside the stadium, had me feeling washed out.

My concern increased after I went over a couple of jumps. I was so shattered that my mind was almost conceding that I was content with my day's work already – *I have a gold medal. Maybe it's not time for me to win another yet.*

Despite these weird thoughts running through my head, I kept warming up, kept flipping over the jumps, and by the end of it I'd reached a decision. I was feeling better, so I figured I might as well do the run I'd planned.

My first attempt was a disaster.

I got through the jumps but didn't execute any of the tricks I'd planned; it was a total forget job. Luckily I had two attempts left.

The second run was a significant improvement, but I still felt I'd missed a couple of tricks, which was why I was pleasantly surprised when I saw my score: 93.00.

'Holy shit, maybe this *is* my time,' I muttered to myself.

Brandon Loupos was the defending dirt champion, and he was in second place with 92.00 after the first two jumps. Suddenly my fatigue disappeared, replaced by excitement and anticipation. If I nailed the run I wanted to do, I was going to be hard to beat.

I was the second-last competitor to go and, with my newfound lease on life, I put together one of the best dirt runs of my life. And the judges loved it, scoring it an impressive 94.66.

The pressure was all on Loupos now, and he clearly knew he had to go for something extra because he pushed it too far on the second jump and crashed. The moment I saw him hit the deck I started cheering and pumping my arms. I was caught in the moment, and I know it's a fine line, but that was my instinctive reaction. Some people have questioned how I could cheer when my mate had just gone down, but I had simply been overcome with emotion at that very moment – I'd just won two X Games gold medals on the same day. And Loupos never took exception or said anything about it.

It was crazy to think it wasn't that long ago that I wasn't even deemed worthy enough to get an invite. Now I was walking away with the ultimate honour and a handy payday of around $100,000. I'd well and truly paid for my home skatepark.

Now my X Games record had a really nice ring to it.

Silver.

Silver. Silver.

Gold. Silver.

And now . . . Gold. Gold.

*

'What are we waiting for?'

It was the question Kim and I started to ask each other. The original plan was to get married after the Olympics, but we had both started to realise there really was no reason to wait. When we got home from the X Games trip to America, the planning began.

When I say 'planning', it's probably more accurate to say 'when my wife-to-be started diving into the logistics'. What I *did* bring to the table was the timing, which we agreed was at the end of November, after the 2019 World Championships in China.

Once again the final stop on the FISE World Series was also held in Chengdu, the week before the world titles, and I was in prime position to claim the overall prize, barring a mishap.

However, that mishap did come, but it wasn't through any fault of my own – chalk it up to the weather gods.

The final was washed out because of heavy rain, which meant the standings after the semifinals stood as the final result. My young Japanese rival, Rim Nakamura, had scored 93.20 points to take the lead, while I was ranked fourth because I'd been holding back in the semifinals to nurse a sore back through the competition. The way I normally ride contests is to keep it chilled during the qualifying rounds – don't do anything special and hold a few things up my sleeve for the final. In this case the issue with my back meant I was playing it safer than normal, but I'd been confident that in the final I'd overhaul the new kid on the block.

I never got the chance, and unfortunately it wasn't going to be the only time luck deserted me on this trip.

Everything had gone smoothly through the qualifying rounds of the world championships until the practice before the final. On my final run-through I popped a tyre, but the problem was that I didn't have time to deal with it since the rider introductions were about to start. So as I was waving to the crowd and keeping a brave face, our team officials were frantically fixing the tyre.

Getting flat tyres is an occupational hazard, but it doesn't happen that often. You always keep an eye on your tyres for signs of wear and tear. Any inkling of a bulge and you swap it out straightaway. Tyre pressure is a personal choice, and all riders are different, with some guys going softer than others. I prefer rock-solid tyres so I can create as much speed as possible, which means I run with a tyre pressure over 100 PSI (pounds per square inch). The maximum you can run is 120 PSI.

With my tyre fixed, I put together a quality run that earned me a nice score of 92.90. In a positive sign for our Olympic qualification campaign, Loupos was my main threat. After stumbling in his first run, my teammate delivered big with his second and final runs, putting up a score of 93.20.

I was the last rider in the competition, and my game plan involved adding a barspin to one trick and a couple of small extras to other parts of my run, which I figured would be enough to boost my score up past Loupos. The first couple of tricks went according to plan, but on the third trick I cased it on the top of the ramp.

It wasn't obvious straightaway, but as I went through the next transition I sensed something was up, and then when I came over the box jump on my next trick my heart sank. I had a flat tyre.

I tried to continue, but the tyre was getting flatter and flatter. There was no other alternative but to stop riding. What are the odds of having *two* flat tyres inside an hour? It just doesn't happen, but unfortunately it had happened in one of the biggest competitions of the year. My chances of another world title were gone.

After the initial anger subsided, there were two things that helped me deal with only getting the silver medal.

With Loupos winning gold, it meant we'd compiled a truckload of rankings points towards the Olympic Games qualification. We'd initially been behind the eight ball after I missed the opening two events of the qualifying period, but we'd now rocketed to the top, where we were tied on the exact same number of points as the United States. Given the pioneer of the sport, Dave Mirra, was American, they understandably held the mantle as the BMX powerhouse, but there were a number of countries where the sport was starting to flourish, including the United Kingdom, Japan and Russia.

The Tokyo Olympics would certainly help determine the pecking order, and it was just crazy that after twelve months of competing it was all square in the race to qualify two riders for the sport's Games debut. It was all going to come down to a couple of competitions in 2020 before the May deadline.

That was exciting, but I had more exciting things in my immediate future, seeing as I was getting married two days after I got home from the world championships.

Our snap decision to bring forward the date had thrown a few curveballs in terms of finding the right place for the ceremony. Kim loves the beach, so she had her heart set on a wedding by the sea. However, the council restrictions in Queensland limiting the number of people and chairs you can have on the beach meant we had to have the ceremony a few kilometres down the road, just over the border in NSW at Kingscliff, south of Tweed Heads.

The reception was held back over the border in Burleigh Heads at a function centre overlooking the ocean. It was a new venue, and as we were finalising the booking they informed us about the 'no visible tattoo' policy. It turns out this was now a thing, where people with tattoos on their hands, neck or face weren't allowed in certain venues.

Given my family's history with body art, this was a deal-breaker. We then found out that the restaurant downstairs at the same venue was owned by different people – people who didn't have the same policy – so we started making enquiries there. The conversation hadn't progressed very far before the reception centre got back to us with a change of heart.

Tattoos were back in.

8

NO PAIN, NO GAIN

Five years. 132 hours. $12,000.

And lots of pain.

Welcome to the Logan Martin tattoo show.

I got my first tattoo when I was sixteen, and it was done by my grandma Raelene. Tattoos were a family business, with my pop, Danny Robinson Snr, a pioneer of the industry in Australia. He passed down his skills to all of his children, including his son, my uncle, Danny 'Nutz' Robinson, who has been in the game for over forty-five years and is revered for his work.

My mum has a sizeable tattoo on her back, and Dad has a few little ones, so it was no surprise that I grew up with an appreciation of body art. My first tattoo came about because I kept nagging Mum while we were at Grandma's house, because she was fixing up a tattoo for my brother. I kept at her all day until she relented. I'm not sure why I chose to have the Southern Cross inked on the inside of my left arm, but I was just a kid who thought it was cool. There was no meaning behind it. I realised later it was a symbol of rebellion and patriotism, but for me in that moment, I just liked the way it looked.

A year later I followed it up with the word 'FAMILY' drawn on my other arm.

When I turned eighteen I decided to get serious about my tattoos. I flew down to Melbourne, where my uncle was based, and the journey began. Over the next five years I would make regular visits, clocking up 132 hours in the chair.

I wasn't planning on getting my full body covered, but I started to enjoy the way it was looking. I had my arms and upper body done first, and then figured it was silly to leave my legs clean.

Each visit to Melbourne would be over two days, and I'd do six- to eight-hour sessions in the chair each day. It was a mental challenge as much as anything else, and there were some areas that still make me cringe thinking about today.

The new tattoos would then be wrapped in cling wrap for three days to help the healing process, which would take around two weeks. During that time, you had to keep the ink out of the sun. You couldn't put sunscreen on the area, and you certainly couldn't go swimming.

My uncle specialised in Japanese artwork, so we started with that imagery on my left arm, where colouring over the Southern Cross was the first priority. Then we carried the theme over to the right arm, before we decided to continue it across my whole upper body. Again, it wasn't about meaning for me; it was all just about looking cool.

On my chest I have a samurai with little demons around it, and on my back there is a large Tibetan skull. For the legs we decided to mix it up, and this was where my love of horror movies got involved. Below each knee are characters from horror movies, including Chucky and his bride, Jigsaw, Annabelle, Freddy and Jason.

I'm not entirely sure where my affection for horror movies came from, but when I was younger I found I never really got scared or jumpy in movies. The storylines in horror flicks and how they came up with the characters were what really intrigued me. I was particularly taken by the Saw series of movies, which were made by Australian filmmakers and followed the work of fictional serial killer John 'Jigsaw' Kramer.

Given Kim isn't a horror movie fan I haven't watched as many in recent times, but I'm glad my secret pleasure plays a significant role in my body art. I even continued the scary theme for the top half of my legs, this time with menacing-looking animals. The iconic giant gorilla King Kong is on one thigh; a large picture of a wolf is on the other.

My final session was on my backside, with the two butt cheeks taking two days. On one side there is another Tibetan skull, similar to what is on my back, with the Buddha on the other one.

And that's it.

I never wanted any tattoos on my hands, neck, face or feet. That was my thing – I didn't want to be that bold with my tattoos and, really, I just didn't want to look like a thug. I can completely cover up if I want to; if I wear a suit you wouldn't know I have any tattoos.

Now let's talk about the pain.

Most sessions had a particular spot that would cause considerable pain. The stomach is a tough one, particularly when he was doing the outline, going down the sternum into my abdomen. You are supposed to stay calm and relaxed, but my stomach would always tense up. And then down on the hip bone area, there would be these crazy vibrations.

The armpits weren't much fun either. There was an intense burning sensation, but I wasn't in the best shape for that session. The night before I'd got food poisoning, so I hadn't had any breakfast because I was feeling so off. That sitting went for four hours, and by the end of it I had hot and cold sweats and was shaking. It was a very bad experience.

But the crème de la crème in the pain stakes were my nipples. It was super quick in terms of duration, probably around ten minutes all up, but because of the tight bundle of nerve endings attached to the areas, it was the most intense pain I'd ever experienced.

As the saying goes, 'No pain, no gain.' I certainly lived that motto during the five years devoted to my body art. The experience cost me around $12,000, which was a discounted rate from my uncle, who did my first arm sleeve for free and then charged $100 for every hour in the chair.

I stopped when I was twenty-three, and I had no intention of getting any more until I had a life-changing experience that required a rethink.

9

THE LOCKDOWN SESSIONS

It was the highest prize purse in BMX history.

A select group of international riders had been invited to Japan to take on the locals in the Chimera A-side contest in Nagoya. The winner would take home a cool $130,000, which was significantly higher than anything we'd competed for previously. The X Games had always been the biggest payday at around $75,000 per gold medal.

It was a great way to start 2020, with the competition being held inside the impressive Aichi Sky Expo exhibition centre. Unfortunately, on the day of the finals I came down with some form of illness. I had a really high temperature when I woke up, so I just pumped in the Nurofen to at least get myself feeling able to compete.

Given the high stakes, the competition was intense, and in the end it was a victory for Australia . . . just the other Australian.

Brandon Loupos snared the big prize while I finished third, which wasn't as exciting as we'd initially thought. There was a dramatic sliding scale with the prize money. It was loaded for first place and dropped off significantly after that, with third prize coming in at $7000.

That night I deteriorated again, experiencing hot and cold sweats. It was full-on. I'd heard on the news a couple of weeks earlier that a virus, one that had originated in China, was set to spread around the globe. It was being called COVID-19. I wondered briefly if that was what I'd contracted. Surely not.

More Nurofen was the order of the day, since I was flying straight from Japan to New Zealand for a small dirt contest called Farm Jam. I love New Zealand – it's one of my favourite places to visit, and I'd ridden at this event previously. There wasn't much money involved, but I liked the vibe of 3000 spectators lining the beautiful Otapiri Gorge on the South Island to watch various extreme sports.

By the time I got off the plane I seemed to be cured. It was weird but my mystery bug had virtually disappeared on the flight. While I may have been feeling better, Mother Nature wasn't smiling on us for the event, with gale-force winds whipping through the surrounding hills. It was too much for the freestyle motocross competition, which had to be cancelled, but the BMX freestyle went ahead, although we all had to scale back the tricks.

This was part and parcel of our sport, dealing with weather, be it wind, rain or extreme heat. You had to be able to adapt. Little did we know but we were about to have to adapt to something much bigger – and much more destructive.

On 21 February, the first domino fell.

The FISE World Series event scheduled for Puyang, China, on 8 May was postponed. Three weeks earlier the World Health Organization had declared an 'international public health emergency'. The coronavirus was no longer just centred around China; it was spreading fast through other Asian and European countries.

Next was the World Cup stop in Hiroshima, Japan, which was scheduled for 3 April and was the last major event of the Olympic qualifying period. It was now off, and given that Tokyo was still four months away, everyone had their fingers crossed that this virus thing would pass.

Unfortunately, it didn't.

Every news bulletin was full of stories about COVID-19 and the impact it was having around the world. Lockdowns were becoming more and more prevalent, and each day a major event was getting postponed.

On 24 March my Olympic dream was over. Or at least put on ice for the time being.

The International Olympic Committee announced that the Tokyo Games would be postponed for a year. Given what a mess the qualifying had become with all of the event cancellations, the decision made sense, even though waiting another twelve months sucked.

A couple of days later, FISE announced that they were cancelling all competitions until June, which meant my favourite Montpellier event wasn't happening this year. Thankfully, there was still the X Games in America. Or so I thought.

That hope lasted less than a month, with word coming out of the States at the end of April that the X Games in Minneapolis, scheduled for July, was also not going ahead. This time I was knocked around. I felt lost. I'd always had something to work towards, a reason for all the sacrifices and training, but there was nothing on my radar now.

I had really got into a good training routine and was feeling super positive on the bike, but now I didn't know what to do. *Do I keep training as hard as I have been, or do I take the foot off the gas and relax a bit?*

I was confused.

It was almost like I'd predicted the future by building a skatepark in my backyard.

As COVID-19 swept through Australia, each state was plunged into lockdowns at various stages. Fortunately, Queensland was nowhere near as bad as other states down south like Victoria. There was only a six-week period where things were really clamped down, but even then I was fortunate to not miss a beat – I had a training partner in residence.

It hadn't taken me long to get out of my funk, and having Andy Buckworth staying at my house certainly helped the situation. He'd been blocked from flying back to the United States, where he was now based as a BMX stunt rider with Nitro Circus, which had grown into a worldwide phenomenon. The shows were off the charts – they'd actually started in Brisbane back in 2010 – and were promoted as an

My life on two wheels just happened to start out on three. It was only up from there!

The Logan City Bandits: me and my brother, Nathan, cruising around on our trikes. It would be several years before we graduated to the skatepark in Crestmead.

I got my BMX L plates at an early age. (I don't look too thrilled with the training wheels.)

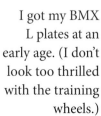

Rugby League was my first sporting passion. Here I am, suited up for the Waterford Mighty Demons.

I didn't shy away from tackling the big kids, and I didn't mind putting a step on them either.

Showing some of the field awareness that made me a good hooker.

I played League until I was twelve, when I was ready to pass the ball off for another sport.

My evolution from the shy kid without much to say to the shy kid without much to say, with aggressive hair. I was ready for the skatepark scene in Crestmead.

First flight: working on my no-handers and tailwhips at the local skatepark in 2009. (Wayne Cant)

A fisheye's view of a barspin. At this stage I was already competing at Core Series events around Brisbane. I won the series twice by the time I was sixteen. (Wayne Cant)

Me as a fresh-faced seventeen-year-old, getting an early overseas break by winning a Gatorade Free Flow Tour event in Greenville, North Carolina, in 2011. Three of the top five riders were Aussies.

Developing the complicated tricks needed to compete on an international level takes hours and hours of practice and discipline – breaking tricks down into parts and putting them all together. Having the flairwhip in my bag at an early age certainly got people's attention.
(Wayne Cant)

Ready to live the dream.
(Wayne Cant)

The dawn of a BMX freestyle career. I was signed on with a sponsor, Sikkair, and getting paid to go overseas and ride my bike. What could be better? (Wayne Cant)

Above: Starting to live the dream. (Wayne Cant)

Left: Even though my speciality is BMX park, I was beginning to hold my own in BMX dirt. Every feature is so much bigger – steeper drop-ins, higher take-offs, bigger down ramps and more air time. Exhibit A. (Wayne Cant)

With a full arsenal of tricks, by 2015 I was ready to take on the X Games, with a vision for gold. Since the only indoor facility in my area shut down, I had to go old school to practise, travelling around to all the local skateparks during the day while the kids were still at school.
(Wayne Cant)

Living the dream.
(Wayne Cant)

A break-through moment – winning silver at the 2016 X Games in Austin, next to American Dennis Enarson (*centre*) and my Aussie mate Kyle Baldock (*right*).

Sharing the joy with Kyle, who went on to win the inaugural Dave Mirra Best Trick contest at the 2016 X Games, in honour of the legend who had passed.

Taking out the 2017 FISE World Championship – and getting that first taste of the Olympic colours around my chest – was an amazing moment. It also proved that I could make a living in BMX.

After a streak of silver, it was time to realise the dream: my first X Games gold in 2018 in Minneapolis, with my partner and best friend Kim by my side.

My luck doubled in 2019 with another gold in BMX park . . . and a gold in dirt! You could say my luck tripled with the addition of Noah to our family.

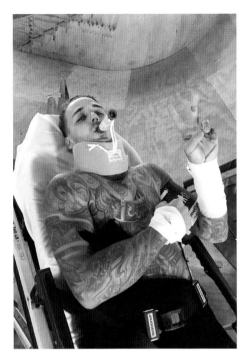
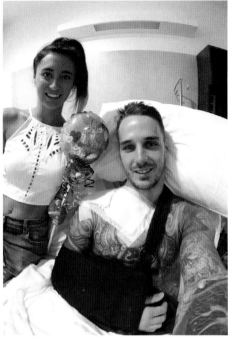

Preparing for an FISE World Tour event in Tokyo in 2018, I came unstuck attempting the highly difficult frontflip flair. Before I knew it I was puffing on the green whistle, bound for the hospital.

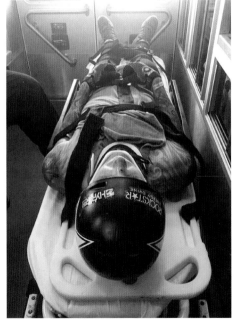

Injuries, concussions, torn ligaments in both ankles, dislocated fingers, bulging discs and broken bones – it's all a part of the BMX freestyle game, and something I've got used to.

Welcome to the Logan Martin tattoo show. The art of tattooing runs deep in my family. My grandmother gave me my first one at sixteen – and I didn't look back from there. From Japanese- and Tibetan-inspired art, to my love of horror movies and menacing animals, my tattoos reflect my journey and passions off the bike. (Thankfully I left room for the Olympic rings.)

Lockdown was hard, but I love a challenge. While building a $90,000 BMX park in your backyard might not be popular with the neighbours, it gave me – and a few of my friends, including Jaie Toohey and Josh Matthews – a chance to stay honed on our mission for Tokyo gold. (Wayne Cant)

Behold, 'Logan Land', Queensland, est. 2019. It's amazing to be able to walk into your yard for a session and some friendly competition.

The view couldn't be better from up here. (Wayne Cant)

2019 was already an epic year, but what a way to top it off, marrying the girl of my dreams on 14 November. Noah clearly couldn't be happier either.

It didn't take long for Noah to share in my BMX journey. He can't get enough of the action outside his window – or travelling abroad to watch me compete around the world.

Taking out the 2021 World Championship at one of my all-time favourite venues in Montpellier, France, was the perfect way to get momentum heading in to the 2021 Tokyo Olympics. I never get tired of raising the flag.

Wade Bootes and AusCycling were true to their word and gave us the best facilities and support in the lead-up to Tokyo. With so much talent in Australian BMX, we were bound to come back with some hardware. (Wayne Cant)

Sharing the Olympic journey with my family and friends, especially Noah, meant the world to me – and I can't wait to see what the next chapter holds.

Post-Olympics saw the birth of my beautiful daughter and final piece to the puzzle, Luna.

My world: Kim, Noah and Luna.

explosive, high-adrenalin action sports spectacular, featuring freestyle motocross, BMX, skate and scooter riders doing crazy tricks.

Similar to the X Games, the Nitro Circus franchise had even created the Nitro World Games, which was another television event. In 2018 I'd travelled to California and managed to add it to my CV with a gold medal in BMX park.

Andy's field of expertise was different to mine – he was more about the bigger, higher jumps. He'd been a regular at X Games in the big air competition, which involved dropping down what was called the 'MegaRamp'. The riders had to actually take an elevator to get to the top of the ramp, which stood twenty-two metres high. It was crazy stuff and not my cup of tea.

Being able to have Andy around meant my routine didn't change. We'd ride each day, and we set up a makeshift gym on my deck as well where we'd work out. At one point the restrictions allowed up to five 'workers' to attend the house, so that meant we could have a couple of my other mates – Jaie Toohey and Josh Matthews – come over and ride also. Technically, I actually did put them to work on the tools to install a fence around my yard.

There was always something that required tinkering at 'Logan Land'. The name had taken off on social media, and it had originated off the back of a couple of other famous extreme sports athletes who'd created their own training facilities. Ryan Williams, an Australian freestyle scooter and BMX rider, had built a large action sports compound on forty acres on the Sunshine Coast, which he called R-Willy Land.

And American action sports legend Travis Pastrana, a moto-cross rider and mastermind of Nitro Circus, had constructed Pastranaland just outside Maryland, which features various jumps all over the property that he says was the driving force behind his daring stunts.

The hot and humid conditions of the Gold Coast caused a few issues at Logan Land. The resi on the ramps started expanding in the sun, making it bubbly with big lumps throughout it. Thankfully, Andy came up with an idea to tighten the resi when it's a hot day and then loosen it in colder conditions. Naturally, we captured the working bee on camera, and it became one of my YouTube specials.

Each day we had a little crew hanging out and riding, which enabled us to tick over while the rest of the world effectively shut down. But there was one major problem: that niggle in the back of my mind about how I wasn't progressing my tricks was still there. The minute Cycling Australia had come on board, they'd always said, 'Just tell us what you need and we'll make it happen.' What we desperately needed was an indoor training facility.

In August 2020, Cycling Australia kept their word.

They leased an empty industrial shed on the Gold Coast for one year and turned it into an indoor skatepark. We'd suspected that COVID might have actually helped us here, since the national organisation would have saved a lot of money in their budgets by not travelling to competitions around the world. These funds were now being directed into helping us get ready for Tokyo.

The closure of GC Compound continued to haunt us. There was an indoor skatepark in Brisbane that was open to the public, and you could ride there if the weather was bad, but it wasn't a training facility. We all contributed to the design of the new park, and Jason Watts, who'd constructed my backyard skatepark, was brought in to build it. There were already some ramps available – which had actually been living in my shed – from a skatepark that had temporarily gone out of business. My mates Shane Smith and Kyle Baldock had gone into the business Level Up Skatepark, and when it closed down during the pandemic they needed somewhere to store the ramps.

The key part of the new set-up was the foam pit. It was crucial for developing our routines. Being able to safely attempt bigger and crazier tricks into the foam, gaining confidence before moving over to the resi, was such an important part of improving ourselves.

It wasn't long before we had a good crew assembled, with the addition of Brandon Loupos, who'd moved from Sydney to the Gold Coast specifically because of the new training facility. Australia's best female rider, Natalya Diehm, who was chasing a spot at the Olympics, was also a regular at the shed, which soon became known as the Hot Box.

There weren't many windows in the building, and the air flow was minimal, so during summer it would get scorching hot. We had also created a little gym in the kitchen area – the room would have been six metres by four metres – and we'd shut all the doors and crank the air conditioner up to 30 degrees to replicate the heat we should expect in Tokyo.

Each day we had a plan.

There were three main tricks I focused on – the double-flair, the switch triple-whip and a front bike flip, which Jaie had been doing for some time.

I'd found out Loupos had been doing the double-flair – which was two backflips with a 180-degree rotation and landing back in the same ramp – on the down-low for a couple of months, and I was keen to learn it also. No-one was doing it in contests, so having that trick at my disposal was going to be a major asset.

The genesis of the switch triple-whip was the 2019 World Championships, where there had been a section of course that you couldn't get enough speed to perform a normal trick on. Doing tricks in the opposite direction – switch – was the future of the sport, and this was a move I could hit over a box jump. It would be a big win for me if I could pull off a switch triple-whip in a spot on the course that my opponents were ignoring because they were worried about speed.

Catching the judges' attention was just as important as doing a clean run. They often wanted to see innovation as much as they liked to see no mistakes.

The switch triple-whip would set me apart, so it was on high rotation in the Hot Box. It was more tactical than anything, whereas the front bike flip was the *Wow* factor you needed up your sleeve. It was a tough trick, and fellow Aussie Ryan Williams had been the first in the world to do one off a big air ramp several years earlier. I'd watched Jaie land it for a while in the normal skatepark format, but I'd been reluctant to embrace it.

However, now that we had a foam pit it was a different story, and having my mate there with me every day to walk me through the intricacies of the trick was an unbelievable advantage.

Without a doubt it was one of the wildest tricks I'd ever attempted, given the bike does a complete flip while you're hovering over the top of it. And then you have to get back onto the bike once it has done its full rotation. There wasn't much control in it because it was all based on the way you let go of the bike and the timing. The problem is it literally feels different every time you attempt it. That's the reason why I'd wavered about taking it on in the past, because to me it was an inconsistent trick.

It's hard to explain the sensation going through you, because for that split second when you release from the bike, it's like, *Alright, here we go!* Then it's up to your hand–eye coordination to figure out when the handlebars are ready to be caught or, if the bars are a little bit too far out of reach, then you adjust accordingly and reel the bike back in.

The first few attempts the bike just went flying into the foam pit. I had to figure out how to keep the bike close to me, even though I'm throwing it forward. There were plenty of spills and lots of face-planting into the foam with the bike whacking me in the head or on my legs.

It probably took me two months doing it every day before I was consistently landing the front bike flip in the foam pit. When I progressed over to the resi, there were a couple of mishaps before I nailed it on the sixth attempt.

I got to test how far I'd come with the front bike flip during our Friday morning competitions, which we'd started as the calendar kicked into 2021.

In an attempt to get our minds and bodies back into competition mode after a year off, we would hold these semi-regular mock events. There were usually five or six of us involved, and we'd treat it like a normal competition, with a thirty-minute warm-up before we'd put down our best one-minute runs.

It was funny. You'd find yourself having the same sort of nerves as in a real competition because you wanted to top your friends. We even had judges – friends or fellow riders who were sitting the session out – to adjudicate.

They compiled scores, and the vibe was pretty intense before we all adjourned outside to have a barbecue, where the winner was announced and given their prize . . . the biggest piece of salmon.

JAIE TOOHEY

Australian BMX rider

Best mate

I'm originally from Newcastle but moved to America when I was pretty young and lived in Greenville, North Carolina. That was where Logan started coming overseas. They called it Pro Town, USA, because Dave Mirra and Ryan Nyquist had their own seperate training warehouses there. There were heaps of Australians who flew out to be a part of that ride, and the other day I came across a photo of twelve Australians lined up against a wall, and you can see how young Logan was. I had met Logan before, back when there were contests around Brisbane when we were younger, but I'd never really spent too much time with him.

It wasn't until I made the move to the Gold Coast that we started spending a lot of time together and became best friends, pretty much doing everything together. That was about seven years ago, right at the time when Nitro Circus started. That was one of the main reasons why I came back to Australia. We were getting really busy with shows, and when I had a break I would rather be at home than living in Greenville.

There was nowhere to ride where I lived with my parents, so I moved up to the Gold Coast – that's where everyone is. It was the best decision, to be around Logan every day, since that was when I started to get back into the contest scene. By that time Logan was real deep in all the FISE competitions, and he was doing so well, winning and winning. That's what made me get back into the competitions, being around Logan.

It's crazy because I still remember those years when we were young, living in Greenville. He did drink then and we had a great time, but then he just completely saw what it was going to take to get to the top. It was almost like he *knew* what he had to do. When he started going to all these FISE competitions and realised what it was going to take, that's when he stopped drinking. He went full one-hundred-per-cent mindset. From then on, and it's been a long time now, he's been the number-one guy. He is the most consistent, he can do everything, and he still has more to do. He just has the strongest mentality. He gets set on what he wants to do and what he needs to do.

If we are going to go to a session and no-one else there wants to ride, he doesn't care if he rides by himself. He is set on that one thing. I think that's why he has got to where he is today: he has not let anything get in the way, and if something does, he finds a way to overcome it, to get around it.

Building the skatepark in his backyard was such a smart investment in himself and had a massive impact on what happened later on. When COVID hit, for that two-year period or whatever it was, we were so lucky to have that skatepark to be able to ride on a daily basis. Even those times when you weren't allowed to leave your house or anything, we were fortunate to have that to ride – most riders weren't allowed to go to a skatepark or anything.

Then the Hot Box was a massive investment by AusCycling that has helped Logan so much as well. While we had Logan's house, which had all the resi, a box jump to a FISE World Cup height and the quarters, all the bigger transitions and everything, the one thing that was missing was a foam pit for Logan to learn all these new tricks. Without that, it would have been a lot harder for him to learn some of the stuff he has now that a lot of people haven't seen.

I had been able to do the front bike flip for a while, and I knew Logan could do it. It's the situation with him that when he figures out a new trick, and does it perfectly, he then pretty much goes out and does it perfectly every time. Sure enough, that's exactly what happened. Whereas if I learn something, I'm just going to go and do it. Even if I'm not one hundred per cent, I'm going to try it anyway. But he's a real perfectionist with everything he does. He won't turn up to a contest, drop in and just wing it – he'll spend weeks and months until he knows he's ready. He's very, very calculating. He won't learn something and then say, 'Okay, I'm going to send it.'

He had that front bike flip for a while. He was able to do it in the foam pit for a very long time, but until he felt like he *needed* to do it, he didn't pull it out. I remember the first time I was trying to get him to attempt it. He was pretty much able to get back on his pedals, so he pretty much had it. From then on, each time he tried it he just figured it out a bit more and a bit more. Now it's just one of those tricks he can go out and do.

That's another reason why he's successful: when he rides his bike, he doesn't have a day where he says, 'Alright, I'm only going to do this and that today.' He goes out and does all his tricks. That's why he is so successful at events, going to all these competitions and doing so well. He's showing up like he's just going to ride his bike, like he normally does every day, because every day he does these tricks no matter what.

We all knew he could win the Olympics because we all know how good he is. Even in Tokyo, he did a run that he does in his backyard every single day. He didn't even have to dig into a bag of tricks that he'd been working on for the last few years. There are so many he has saved up that he hasn't posted on Instagram. My phone is full of all these tricks that the world has never seen. No-one even knew he could do them except for the people who were around him, and he didn't have to unleash one of them. For him to go there, lay down a run he does every single day and still come away with gold is incredible. If he has to dig deep at some point, there is so much more. I feel like he's definitely not maxing out his runs at the moment.

So many people look up to him. He's the best rider in the world, and he's so professional. You look at the sport now compared to where it was when we lived in Greenville. It was more about the contests that we would get around to back then; we never thought it was going to be an Olympic sport. We just used to have drinks, ride our bikes and have a bit of fun – now you want to be at the top. If you want to be at Logan's level, you can't be going out on weekends and drinking and then come Monday be as fit on your bike. With Logan doing what he does, it's just not possible anymore.

You look at the level of riding from last year to this year – it's only going to get bigger and bigger and bigger. He has made his name in the sport, and I feel like there are so many younger kids coming in now, trying to be like Logan. They just want to be him. They are looking at Logan to see what he can do, trying to do what he does. The kids are getting so good from such a young age, pulling off some of the tricks that Logan does – just imagine where they are going to be down the track. Logan has helped create that younger generation that is going to come up and keep progressing from here on.

10

NO HOLDING BACK

'I'm just going to do this.'

It went against everything I'd done previously, but it had been sixteen months since we'd been at an international competition, and this was no ordinary event. This was the 2021 World Championships and the deciding event for Tokyo Olympic qualification.

All the conservatism of holding back with my first run that had been the hallmark of my career was suddenly getting the flick. I wasn't completely sure why, but I had a different energy on the bike – energy that had clearly been pent up over the long COVID break. I was ready to make my mark.

We'd got word in April that the UCI had pencilled in the world championships at Montpellier, France, for 5–8 June. Finally, we had something to look forward to, although it was going to make things tight given the rescheduled Olympics were now starting in just over a month, on 23 July.

The world was still in the grips of the coronavirus, but there was at least light at the end of the tunnel, with the vaccination roll-out paving the way for us to start getting back to something resembling normality.

It certainly made travelling a whole different ball game, with the layers of testing and preventative measures like full-time mask-wearing and social distancing. We'd been told we had to adhere to the metre-and-a-half rule at the event, so there would be no high-fiving or hugging our mates after they'd finished their run. The new norm was going to be tough, but it was our life moving forward for the foreseeable future.

Australia sent a team of four, which included reigning world champion Brandon Loupos, Jaie Toohey and Josh Matthews. The selection had followed the national championships in Melbourne in March, where I'd won my third consecutive Australian title. These events had only been introduced since AusCycling (formerly Cycling Australia) came on board with the Olympics on the horizon.

There had been a school of thought that we were likely to get two riders selected for Tokyo if there were no more qualifying events. Given Loupos and I had finished in the top two placings at the previous world championships back in 2019, that would ultimately be the deciding factor in our tiebreak with the Americans.

Loupos in particular had been thinking that way, whereas even when it looked like there wouldn't be another competition, I was keeping my head in the game in case there was. We'd have to finish first and second on the podium to both make it to Tokyo.

It hadn't been a great lead-up for my teammate. He'd been dealing with some personal issues that would have been tough at any time, but they were particularly challenging when you're just weeks away from the biggest event of your career.

I'm always trying to look on the positive side, so I figured if he got through the championships he'd have six weeks to clear his mind for the Olympics. There was enough time; he just had to snap into action in Montpellier. Unfortunately, it was obvious it wasn't the same Loupos during practice, and he only just managed to scrape through the semifinals.

He was the first rider to go in the final, and his run started promisingly, but then twenty seconds later disaster struck. He'd just landed a trick on the spine when his right knee gave way. He had to stop immediately, and as I watched my teammate hobble from the course I knew exactly why it had happened.

I was convinced all the stress he'd put on his mind in the lead-up because of the personal issues had played out on the bike. I was shattered for him, but I couldn't go over to console him. I had to stay focused on what I was there to do.

But that became even harder when I watched another one of my mates, Great Britain's Declan Brooks, suffer a horrific crash just a few metres away from where I was standing. It happened towards the end of the run, when he'd attempted a double-backflip but didn't rotate enough. He landed hard on his front wheel and then face-planted into the ground, instantly knocking himself out.

It was a scary moment and, with the stadium empty because no spectators were allowed due to COVID, the sound of the crash echoed through the venue. Officials and paramedics rushed over to Declan because he wasn't moving. It was a tough thing to witness just before your own run, particularly on top of seeing what had also just happened to my Australian teammate.

All I could do was keep telling myself, *Stay focused, stay in the zone*, because there wasn't much I could do to help Declan at that moment. The final was delayed for forty-five minutes as every precaution was taken to ensure he was okay. Accidents are a part of the sport – we all know this – but the intensity of what we'd just witnessed rocked everyone. We had to find a way to put it to one side for the next hour.

I was still strong on my change of plan. Safety was out; big tricks were in. I'd done a front bike flip in practice, which had raised eyebrows among my rivals. They knew it was coming out at some stage.

It actually worked perfectly for the run I'd planned because it was a trick you could do off minimal speed, and there was a transfer on the course where it was going to be difficult to do many tricks. That was my spot to deliver the *Wow* factor, and it couldn't have gone better. I also threw in a 720 barspin, a 1080 and a triple-tailwhip, among other tricks, for an opening run that I was super-pumped with.

According to the judges my punt had paid off: they scored it an impressive 94.90.

As I was digesting that result, I realised Loupos was going to try and get back on his bike for a second run.

'Mate, your health is more important,' I said. 'You don't want to make things worse with your knee than they already are.'

photos in this section courtesy Wayne Cant)

He wasn't interested in my advice.

'I want this so bad. I want to get to the Olympics,' were his parting words before he pedalled onto the course again.

I could see on his face he didn't believe it himself, and we were all holding our breath when he dropped in and did a backflip on the box as his first trick. As soon as he landed it, Loupos stopped riding. His knee was no good; his Olympic dream was over.

Again, I found myself being forced to put my concern for him aside and focus on my job. I was leading going into the second round, but that didn't mean anything given the world championship format was two one-minute runs in the final with the highest scoring run counting.

I'd decided to make a tactical change and mix things up for the second run, with the main difference being I wasn't going to do the front bike flip again. There were plenty of other big-scoring tricks left in the bag, including a switch triple-whip, which I'd never done before in a contest. That's why when my minute was up I thought I'd produced an even better run than my first.

I was expecting 95-point-something, so when the scoreboard flashed up a 93.30, I was a bit surprised. However, it didn't take me long to realise they were sending a message to me for the six weeks until Tokyo. The judges had clearly enjoyed the front bike flip and bumped my score up accordingly, which meant the smart move was to make sure I pulled it out at the Olympics.

There were two more riders left in the competition, so it was an anxious few minutes' wait while the American pair, Nick

Bruce and Daniel Sandoval, did their runs. Thankfully, they didn't do enough and I was crowned the 2021 world champion.

More importantly, I was going to the Olympic Games.

Sadly, though, I would be on my own, given Loupos's unfortunate accident meant the US had won the right to take two riders after Justin Dowell and Nick Bruce finished fourth and fifth. Strangely, Sandoval, who had really emerged, was only going to Tokyo as an alternate. I considered him the best of the Americans.

On the Australian front, Josh Matthews had done well to finish sixth, and Jaie Toohey recovered after crashing out in his first run to finish tenth.

It was an awkward trip home for the Australian team, given the agony and ecstasy we'd experienced. Loupos was understandably gutted, while I was in the seat next to him beaming. Our relationship is an interesting one – we're mates, but I get the sense he sees me more as a competitor than a friend.

We broke out into the scene at the same time, and he took a little bit longer to start winning but obviously then quickly established himself as one of the best BMX athletes in the world. We have the same friend group, but at times there is a weird vibe between us, which is probably because we are often fighting for the same thing.

On the plane I didn't really go too deep into things with him. I figured he needed some time to digest what had just happened. And time was something we were both about to have in abundance.

*

They couldn't have found a worse room if they'd tried.

For two weeks I had to live in what I'm tipping was the smallest room at Brisbane's Novotel, the hotel where I was serving out my quarantine period after returning from France.

It was barely four metres by four metres in size, and the window didn't open, so there wasn't a hint of fresh air. The one positive was that it faced the right direction and the sun was shining in all day. I spent a lot of the time looking out the window at the big field below, the daily mowing of the lawn keeping me fascinated.

My food intake would be all delivered via Uber Eats, so at least I was able to maintain some healthy eating habits. For my fitness, I had an assault bike and weights delivered to the room. My workouts were all about testing my mind. I'd flog myself for an hour on the bike and see how many calories I could burn, and then I'd try to beat that number the next day.

I was able to stick close to my normal gym routine, where I would work on mobility with stretching. I needed to keep up my strength and make sure my muscles were ready to handle getting straight back on the bike for what was set to be an intense four-week training block. The special part? A replica of the Tokyo Olympic course had been built on the Gold Coast and was waiting for me the moment I was released from quarantine.

I still couldn't believe it had happened, but when Cycling Australia said they were 'there to help', they weren't joking. Wade Bootes had been very clear in his message about the new training facility.

'I don't care what happens after it. I want you to ride it for four weeks and go to the Olympics with practice and confidence,' he said.

It was a $300,000 investment, which blew my mind, and it had only come about a couple of months earlier when the scheduled test event on the Tokyo course was cancelled. It was actually my old rival, Daniel Dhers, who'd helped make the replica course possible.

He was part of an advisory group that had been working with the Tokyo officials setting up the competition, and when the test event was canned he lobbied for the course design to be released. The theory was that if the test event had happened, all the riders would have obviously had the opportunity to scope out the course. This way, they would at least have a general idea of the layout.

The officials probably weren't expecting a country to build a temporary course, but AusCycling moved fast when they were provided with the information and specs.

'Are you crazy? That's a big job. It's going to cost a lot of money,' was my first reaction when Wade had raised the idea.

The approval soon came from further up the management chain, and a week later they'd picked out the site and had the timber delivered. Jason Watts, who'd built my skatepark, was employed to copy the Tokyo model, with a crew of twelve brought in to make it happen quickly.

This was prior to the world championships and before Loupos's injury, so at that stage AusCycling figured both of us would be going to the Olympics and that the chance of one of us winning the gold medal was very strong. We were both world champions and X Games gold medallists, and having two of the nine riders in the competition were odds they liked.

Thankfully it was a punt they were willing to take in pursuit of a gold medal.

The park was built about fifteen minutes from my house at Carrara, alongside Metricon Stadium, which was the home of the AFL's Gold Coast Suns.

When I got my freedom, and after reuniting with Kim and Noah, I quickly made my way to my new playground. I still couldn't believe it, even as I was riding around the park. My first impression was that it was tougher than I'd expected. My brain was going at a hundred miles an hour, trying to figure out what tricks would work where. Some of my bigger tricks might not be suited to the layout, including the front bike flip and switch triple-whip, which I had spent so long developing.

Joining me every day on the course was Australia's female representative and fellow Queenslander Natalya Diehm, who had trained with us back at the Hot Box. Natalya had emerged as the country's leading female rider back in 2019, winning overseas and then taking out the Oceania and national titles. She then finished sixth on her Australian team debut at the world championships.

Natalya agreed that it was a challenging course – and things were about to get a lot more challenging for her a couple of weeks out from departure.

She'd had a history of knee problems, and during one of our training sessions she blew out her ACL for the fifth time. Given her history and experience with the injury, she decided to not tell anyone and back herself to fight through the pain in Tokyo. Too much hard work had gone into the journey.

It was gutsy and inspiring stuff.

There were no such scares during my practice stint, and the day before I was scheduled to fly out to the Olympic Games I had one last spin around for good measure. It was only good vibes. I had that confidence Bootes had requested . . . by the bucketload.

The successful training block wasn't the only thing that was putting a smile on my face – Kim and I had it confirmed that she was pregnant with our second child. It was a relief as much as anything, because we'd unexpectedly had trouble conceiving No. 2. Kim had fallen pregnant and was feeling sick, showing all the normal signs, but at the eight-week mark it was diagnosed as an ectopic pregnancy.

We were shattered. Then the doctors found some cysts on her ovaries, which required more surgery. It was emotionally tough, given we'd had no trouble with Noah. We figured, since we were both fit and healthy, didn't drink or smoke, that conceiving again wouldn't be an issue.

Our focus was then to make sure Kim recovered and was healthy, and it took more than six months before we were cleared to try again. Then when that didn't go how we'd planned initially, there was more stress. Thankfully, though, we finally got the good news.

I was hoping this was a sign of good things to come in 2021.

WADE BOOTES

Technical Director, BMX

AusCycling

We knew of the BMX freestyle component but we weren't really associated, so it came as a shock when the IOC (International Olympic Committee) announced that freestyle was in the 2020 Olympics. It was like, oh shit. I went straight to Google: right, who do we have in Australia? Actually, we've got Logan; we've got Kyle Baldock; we've got all of these guys. That's where it started, and the biggest challenge for me post 2017 was with a new director, as most of the investment went into track cycling. We sort of got a reduction from BMX race, and then freestyle was added after all the financial things were set up. Now I had to set up two disciplines with half the money that I used to have.

I had to convince the director and CEO back in the day to actually allow us to go and sign these guys up to the first world championships. Upper management was saying, 'Budgets are thin, plans are set out, this is what we are doing.' I said, 'Guys, we have to do freestyle.' An that's when Logan won that world championship.

So it took a lot of convincing, and from then on we had to make some tough calls. There was no additional injection of money from the AIS (Australian Institute of Sport). We had to, as a sport, decide on priorities, and when you come back to mathematics, when nine people start at the Olympics and there are three chances to win a medal, that's pretty damn good odds. I used that whole *Moneyball* philosophy. It just comes back to objectives, common sense and mathematics, to say, 'Well, hey, there is a greater probability – not that I'm not going to guarantee it – that if I put my energy into this then we could come away with two medals.'

Then I had to reach out to Logan, and it was like, 'Hey, Logan, I'm the guy from BMX. There are Olympics now – would you even be interested?' That's how I had to start the relationship, and then my role was to start to educate the whole freestyle world on how a sanctioned sport in the Olympics works and how to qualify for it. It's not because you have a Rockstar sponsorship and you go to the X Games. You have to do the sport process, and there is a lot of education.

It took a bit for Logan to buy in, and then he started to realise we were only there to help and assist versus take over. We weren't going to over-coach and over-direct; we were just going to say, 'Hey, this is what is required. How are we going to make it happen?' To get that buy-in we explained we had to do these C1 events, we had to do these World Cup events, and then you start applying performance behaviours.

You have got super-talented athletes, but then the whole performance mindset comes around: where and how do we structure events so you don't have your resting period when you're injured all the time. That is how they rode – *ride, ride, ride, oh, I hurt myself because I'm tired, and now I have a week off.* That's where we have implemented a lot of the performance behaviours. We're not a high-performance program. We are doing basic education for super-talented athletes, and then hopefully we start engraining more scientific evidence, but we cannot take away the art of coaching or the art of their discipline. That's what I keep telling these guys and reminding them: you guys are the artists; you are the performers with athletic ability. What they do is art. My role is to make sure we still encourage the creativity of these talented athletes by providing a little bit more of a best-practice approach, but we have to let them drive it.

At the X Games, these guys are taken care of – there is a hotel next to the venue, there is a whole athlete lounge, they have got physiotherapists if they get sore. They have it pretty good on those components. Then you come back to us – there is no food and catering trucks for these guys. 'Sorry, we have to make our own sandwiches today.' It's a little bit different, but I think they appreciate the energy that goes on behind the scenes that allows them to do their performance.

We are just a support avenue – we're not your maids, not your mum and dad. If something goes wrong with your bike, we are fixing it. If something goes wrong with your body, we are fixing it. They have a lot of the self-coaching, peer coaching, or they're egging each other on. That's the culture of extreme sports, of lifestyle sports, and I think that's the culture we are maintaining here. We're trying to replicate the peer coaching, because that's how they learn. If they tell someone how to do a trick, then they are actually learning how to do it better anyway.

We've watched, listened and guided a little bit. When we first had a plan for Logan to go down to Adelaide to our head office, it's not rocket science what we were trying to do. We were just doing fundamental movement patterns to help the ankle move. They complain about this and that; we've got to enhance their eccentric loading (creating muscle elasticity to produce force) because all these guys do is land. We need to enhance their range of motion, to have more strength and minimise injury.

Logan would train a shitload, get tired and fatigued, fall over and hurt himself or stress out his lower back, because he is doing fifty thousand things in a day. If you just balance this out, you can actually get more for less. I think he has definitely taken that on board, especially now that he is getting older, and there is a little bit more routine and structure because he has kids now.

The normal coaching principles say development is all about technical, then tactical, then physical, mental and life balance. For Logan's top end it is the other way – you have to have a life-balance component first so you can recover well so you can train well and then make good tactical decisions to then actually get better. If we don't get the life balance right with the top-end athletes, it ain't going to work. But for a development athlete you have to educate them on how to do a barspin, because they are working it out. That's been fun as well. It's just managing the complexity of what is required, what is best practice, how we better prepare and plan for upcoming events and being specific in some areas. Riding the concrete bowls before the X Games, doing some dirt riding before the X Games – that's how we are assisting.

The other thing we provide is a training environment or a training facility to enhance what the athletes used to try and do in kids parks. A lot has changed since 2017 when the Olympics were announced. There is a lot of potential for longevity for a lot of these guys' careers if they plan it out well.

It just comes back to the performance planning, seeing where the gaps are. When we asked what they needed to go to the next level, they didn't have a foam pit. All skateparks were closed down because of COVID, and there were no foam pits. The question became, 'What do we have to do to make this happen?' COVID was actually a huge blessing for us, keeping in mind we weren't very well supported, only because no-one could travel. So we came up with a plan that could actually enhance an outcome, because it is all about pitching and lobbying and working the stakeholders to say building an indoor facility is probably a good idea.

Then we brought in the CEO of QIS (Queensland Institute of Sport) and the AIS to check out the new facility that we'd built. That brought on more support. And when we had the chance to build the replica of the Tokyo Olympic course, everybody was in. With that one it was the Gold Coast Council, Queensland Institute of Sport and Australian Institute of Sport all pulling things together for a performance outcome, and if you can refer things back to an outcome to assist performance, then there is pretty good buy-in.

Building the replica all started at the national championships in March 2021. We had a new CEO come down and watch an event for the first time. We had our performance director show up for the first time. They were like, 'Oh, I didn't know it was this cool.' From that night we had a conversation with Jason Watt, who helped us build the Coomera indoor facility. We just threw it out there: 'Hey, what would it cost to put in a replica? What would be the total cost?' We had those types of discussions that night at the national championships.

I knew the drawings of the Tokyo course were coming out on 1 April. The UCI (Union Cycliste Internationale) try and hold things off so no-one can do what we did. In the process, prior to that I had negotiations with Hurricane (urban sports and entertainment group) to try to start buying a proper Hurricane course, but we knew it wasn't going to land in Australia in time. It got to the point where the performance director was going to the board of AusCycling and saying, 'Hey, do you want to spend $250,000 on a replica course for five weeks?' And we got that approved, with some contribution from QIS and AIS, so it wasn't just all AusCycling. Then in between those two weeks before the drawings were released, we were like, 'Where are we going to put this thing?' The QIS was going to give us their parking lot up at Brisbane. Then during the conversation with the Gold Coast council, they were like, 'Why don't we put it on this piece of grass at Carrara?' And then you pay for the replacement of the grass, which was going to be $10,000. We thought, perfect, just put it there.

Then from 1 April Jason had the drawings, and it was all about quoting how much wood we'd need. I had to research where to get the ten kilometres of framing wood that we needed to buy. So here's me going in saying we need ten kilometres of this wood, and they're all like, 'We can't make that order – there's not enough wood in the Gold Coast for that.' Bunnings, however, did make it happen, and we spent $110,000 just on wood. Then it was a matter of coordinating everything – doing the project plan with Jason, measuring it all out to make sure the course fit. I think it was May when we started building, so it all happened so damn quick, getting approvals and paying Bunnings to get the thing happening.

Then during that period the UCI said, 'We're going to put a world championship on in June now; it's going to be the last qualification for the Olympics.' We were then like, 'Oh my God, we're going to build this thing and we might not get to ride it.' That was my fear: *we've spent a quarter of a million dollars and we're going to be stuck in quarantine on the way home.*

So we had already started to build it, and then we had to go to France to try and qualify for the two spots, which unfortunately we didn't secure, since Brandon Loupos did his ACL. Natalya Diehm got to ride it while we were overseas; there was no benefit to her going to the worlds because she had already qualified. Then Logan had his four and a half weeks on the course, which, when you think about it, athletes get maybe eight hours of practice all week on the course at the

Olympics. He had four weeks on the replica, so that was huge. Even if we only had a week, I think the quarter of a million dollars would have been well spent to get there. We did it the cheapest way possible. We got the cheapest plywood, since we knew it was just going to be a short-term component.

When we got to Tokyo it was pretty cruisy. It's simple once you get into the village; it's simple when you know what you have to get done. You don't have all the external drama; it's all just about daily activity – get ready for tomorrow and focus on the process. We had a strategy that we weren't going to overtrain during the week, just to make sure we were primed for the day of competition. We had a clear plan of what we were doing in practice for Logan and Natalya.

Logan was very superstitious in everything he did. He wouldn't adapt a lot, like changing his back wheel at one world championship. He had a spare wheel but he wanted the other tyre on that wheel, so when he got a flat tyre, we were like, 'Can't we put the spare wheel on? That's why it's there.' But that's how he was – he wanted certain things a certain way – but at the Olympics something went wrong with his bike and he adapted to new behaviours. We had a good spare wheel, we put it on, and he ended up competing on that spare wheel. That led to him adapting to situations but also to focusing on other things that helped his performance during the day. He embraced being under the umbrella, whereas the other guys were like, 'It's too cool to be under the umbrella.' He started using performance behaviours that better prepared him as an athlete so he could do his thing.

His strategy is always about having a clean first run to get a medal – that is his focus, that is why he is so damn consistent. He runs his B game first to say, 'Yep, I'm one hundred per cent I can get this B line together, and it's probably going to get me a medal.' And then he comes out with the additional tricks in the second run to try and land that win. I think he was more advanced than everybody at the Olympics, with the opposite tricks and all of the other components, although I was just so gutted for him that he didn't actually get to show his true potential in that last run. It would have been a 99.9.

When I explain why Logan is the best, I say it's that he is more of an athlete who rides a bike, whereas some freestylers are just talented and get away with just riding the bike. Logan likes to be athletic, he likes to train, he likes to do the process, he likes to do the work to get an outcome. He has mentioned it a couple of times when talking about competitions. He did simple competitions when he first started at fourteen and fifteen for the purpose of getting better at competitions. That's just a clear, simple tactic and strategy. *I'm going to do this shitty little competition, but I want to get better at competitions so I can dominate when I go overseas.*

I think that is the drive. It's all internal. He's got internal motivation – he's not depending on the external motivation of a prize, or somebody egging him on or trying to motivate him. He has the drive to be the best he can be and to keep learning. It was the same thing when he grew up. It was all about riders riding together, but I think he just went, *Far out, I can do something good if I do this really good.* He may not have been as talented when he first started, but it's the work ethic, the commitment that overtakes all these talented people who ride bikes. I think he's got that high level of commitment, that work ethic. Combine that with good talent, and that's the formula for creating a superstar.

He thought he was pretty well known in the industry of freestyle. I think he's like, *Oh my God, there is another whole world out there from the Olympic component.* I don't think he could believe the real support that was coming in. As a sponsored athlete he got all this stuff and got some fans, but when you become a household name and people actually want to take up BMX freestyle because of you, then that's an impact, that's a legacy. I think having somebody like that who is grounded and will help, versus the opposite, is important. He is still going to get on with his daily life, still assist the sport to grow and still be a great role model for sport, for action sport, for activity – all these good words – but to have a good human doing that is the important thing.

I'm so happy for what Logan has achieved. I'm trying to get him to the LA Olympics in 2028. I said, 'Mate, you've got plenty of years left, if you can balance this out.' And I know in his mind if he doesn't want to do it or can't have a chance of getting a good result, he is a person who will step away. That's basically what I did – I gave up on the Olympics to coach. I could have got the T-shirt, but I knew I wasn't going to get a medal. So I'm going to try and keep him going as long as he can and have a great career, and hopefully a post-career that gets him into the coaching space as well.

A hell of a lot has happened in the last five years. We've won three out of the four world champion-ships. We've won the only Olympic gold medal. We've got four athletes in the finals at the last world cham-pionships, so it's not just Logan who is benefitting. Hopefully that's the legacy we've built and left behind now, and having Logan is such a good asset – as a role model, a communicator, an advocate. We just have to get more people on board to say, 'Let's go. Action sport is coming.'

11

TOP OF THE WORLD

'Don't change anything you have ever done.'

My wife's words were front of mind as I landed in Tokyo and began the long process of getting through the airport's exhaustive COVID protocols. It was the new world, and it called for patience.

Kim had made a lot of sense.

The key to being successful at the Olympic Games is to not think about it as the Olympic Games. It's just another major event, like the many I'd competed in over the past eight years.

'Don't think of it as anything bigger,' she said.

I'd won world championships and X Games; they hadn't been flukes. I'd produced my best when the pressure was at its highest. Tokyo was going to be no different. My calling card was my strength of mind – it had been that way since back when I was a teenager – so I just had to flick the switch now and focus on what I could control.

All the training was done, all the hard work had been put in. Now I just had to add the performance element.

There was a great vibe about the athletes' village when we arrived. The rooms were small and the recyclable cardboard beds that had been talked about a lot in the media leading in seemed to do the job.

I was rooming with another BMX guy, racer Anthony Dean, and this was his third Olympic Games. He'd been an alternate in 2012 in London but competed at Rio four years later. I'd got to know him previously, so he was pretty chilled and we just both went about doing our own thing.

The BMX freestyle schedule couldn't have worked out any better given the qualifying and finals were down for a 12 pm start, which was 10 am in Australia – the exact time I usually rode when I was back home. This meant nothing really changed in my routine. I could eat, sleep and ride on the same schedule as I did back home.

A predicted, it was also very hot and humid in Tokyo, which again worked in my favour because I loved riding in the heat. I enjoyed sweating a lot, and that's exactly what was going to be happening at these Olympics. As well as training in high temperatures, I'd actually been going to a sauna back home during the four-week training block to get my body prepared for the extreme conditions.

There were four practice sessions leading into Saturday's seeding round, and then the final on Sunday consisted of two runs, with the best score winning gold.

Understandably, there was a high level of anticipation among all the riders about the first look at the Ariake Urban

Sports Park course. And I think I was the one smiling the most after the first practice session.

'I'm on here,' were the words which came out of my mouth after my first drop-in.

It felt better than the Gold Coast replica but had that level of familiarity about it, which I knew was such an advantage. There were some slight differences, given we didn't have the exact measurements for the transitions or distances between the jumps. We'd built the course simply off a picture and tried to copy it.

But even these adjustments were making our life easier rather than harder. Part of my planned run was a backflip with a tailwhip over a transfer, but back home I was finding it quite hard, as the spine was fairly steep. Not in Tokyo; the transfer was actually bigger, which made it a much mellower transition, meaning it was easier to control the pop range and easier to land.

That's why I was so excited after the first practice session. The real course was easier than the replica, and I was in my element. I already knew my line and what tricks I would be doing, so the next three days was all about repetition, going over the same line with the same tricks just to get even more comfortable.

Word had filtered out about the Gold Coast training course. The Americans and English seemed to have a particular awareness about it, but I wasn't giving anything away. In fact, I put it back on them, as I'd heard they'd done the same thing. It really didn't matter, given everyone is going to do their own thing on the course. They're not going to copy what I'm putting down because I have my strengths and they are better at different things.

What I *did* like about it was the fact it was playing on their minds. That made me smile, which was something I was already doing a lot of in Tokyo.

The gust of wind seemed to come out of nowhere.

When you're in the middle of a 1080, that's not the ideal scenario. It threw me out a bit, and as a result I under-rotated on the trick and hit the deck hard on my hip. I quickly bounced up and shrugged off the minor mishap. If you were doing a scale of the crashes I'd had in my career, it would barely rate a mention.

However, I didn't attempt the trick again during that session and decided it would be smarter to come back in twenty-four hours and do it again. At this stage I wasn't planning to pull it out on my first run in the final, but it would be central to my all-or-nothing second run to grab the gold medal.

Getting treatment for my sore hip was the immediate priority – an ice bath and a constant stream of anti-inflammatory tablets the key to ensuring it wouldn't be an issue. And it worked. Much to my surprise, I woke up the following morning and the hip wasn't too bad.

The debrief on the crash had me convinced that it was all about the wind; I knew what I had to do. If the wind wasn't a factor in the next practice session, I would focus on getting my confidence back and perform the 1080 just like I planned on Sunday.

That was a good approach, but I didn't factor in the weather gods intervening again.

Five minutes into Friday's final practice session we were all looking to the sky, where flashes of lightning and claps of thunder were breaking out across Tokyo. That was enough for the Games officials to cancel the session, which left me with a dilemma. I hadn't had the opportunity to do another 1080, so there was that very small seed of doubt still lingering from the crash.

The 1080 wasn't required for Saturday's seeding run, where everyone normally holds back their big numbers, preferring a more conservative approach. It was meant to be a walk in the park, but when I woke up the most nervous I'd been in a long time, my anxiety shot through the roof. I was so nervous that at one stage I was literally shaking.

I couldn't eat breakfast, which is so rare for me. This sort of episode hadn't happened since my very early days on the tour, and yet here I was at the biggest event of my life and I was losing it.

Eventually, I forced myself to have some food, since I knew I needed something in my stomach for energy purposes, but I was totally freaked out by what was happening. All I could think was, *If this is anything like how I'm going to feel tomorrow, then I'm in big trouble.*

Getting on my bike was the only thing that seemed to calm the nerves. That was clearly the place where I was the most comfortable, and as I went through my warm-up I finally started to feel something approaching normal again.

With only nine riders it was a smaller than normal field, so the qualifying didn't take long. We had two runs each and there was nothing too fancy in terms of big-time tricks being pulled out, but, importantly, I was smooth, clean and riding at a pretty high standard according to the judges. They scored my best run 91.90.

That was enough for first place – no other rider had scored over 90 – which meant I'd be riding last in the final. Earlier in my career, when I was trying to build my reputation, I'd put a lot more emphasis on qualifying and trying to get the number one spot, but that wasn't the case now. Although, I didn't mind having that ranking going into the sport's first ever Olympic final.

Kim's words of advice had been a constant reference point during the week, and they were getting another run around as I lay in bed that night, unsuccessfully trying to get to sleep, constantly worrying about the state I'd be in when I woke up. It was a weird scenario.

'Don't make this bigger than anything else you've done,' was on high rotation.

Eventually sleep came, and when I did wake I braced myself for those same feelings from twenty-four hours earlier to hit. Thankfully, they didn't come, and initially *that* felt kind of weird. I'd built worries up so much that when the nerves weren't there it was odd. I went through my normal morning routine, and when breakfast wasn't an issue I decided it was time to embrace the change.

Clearly it was a good sign that I was back to feeling at the top of my game. I'd got the nerves out of the way the previous day, and now I was as ready as I could be. The whole week in Tokyo couldn't have gone better, really, with the minor crash on Thursday a distant memory.

Most importantly, I was feeling good on the bike and was very comfortable with the course. They were the only two big ticks I needed.

The strategy for my opening run in the Olympic final had been tossed around for months, but the events of the week had solidified my belief that a conservative approach was best. There would be no 1080 or a front bike flip, which had been my highest scoring trick at the world championships.

But I would be doing my signature trick – the switch triple-whip, which no-one else was doing in competition.

It was a trick I'd practised during the COVID break, and it came about off the back of the 2019 World Championships, where there was an obstacle on the course that I couldn't quite get enough speed for, so I had to settle for a trick that wasn't as big as I wanted it to be.

This had driven me mad, so when I got home I was, like, 'Right, what trick can score really well if I don't have enough speed?'

Then it came to me: *Why don't I do the triple-whip the opposite way?* It was almost like writing with your opposite hand, and it took a couple of months to build my confidence. Every day in practice I'd be refining the movements because I wanted to get it to the point where it felt like a common trick. Doing tricks the opposite way was the direction the sport was quickly heading in.

I knew from the recent world championships, where I did both the normal triple-whip and the switch triple-whip, that they were high-scoring moves. It showed diversity, which the judges were always looking for.

All I wanted to do with my first run was put a decent score on the board, and if I executed what I'd planned cleanly, the most likely score would be around the 90–91-point mark.

The key was starting big. When I'd seen the layout of the course, I realised there was a spine straight into a box jump, then a transfer to a wall, but you could only get to the wall transfer if you'd landed at the top of the ramp with speed from the previous jump. These are the types of calculations that continually occupy your mind in the lead-up to a competition. I knew I could score well on this course if I could do two tricks on the spine and the box and then still do a trick into the transfer.

This meant I had to scale down some tricks in order to have enough speed to make the jump and corresponding transfers. One of my strengths was doing a flipwhip transfer over something, and on this course there was one particularly tricky spot where there was a six-foot gap across a spine with nothing in the middle.

Not many of my competitors were hitting it, so I thought this was a perfect opportunity to capitalise. The key was finding my strengths on the course where I could do high-scoring tricks but always ensure I landed with speed to get to the next jump and keep the whole line flowing well.

The run I'd planned had what I would describe as medium-sized tricks, but my point of difference was that it packed a lot more in certain parts of the course, which the judges liked to see. It's funny how all these years of training and competing comes down to a one-minute performance.

Luckily I wasn't thinking like that as I dropped in and went big early with a 720 barspin on the spine, which I followed with a barrel-roll barspin on the box.

From there I was locked in and everything started the flow with an array of tailwhips, flair barspins and a frontflip no-hander. There were no bobbles – or casing, as we call it, where you do a jump and hang your back wheel on the top of the ramp, which means you lose a bit of speed and have to pedal out of it to get back on pace. It's an obvious sign to the judges, the same with landing a jump and your foot slipping off the pedal. That's another no-no and a points reduction.

There were no such issues on my run, which was pretty flawless, and immediately my head went to the parts of the course I would be inserting the bigger jumps into during the second run.

Then I saw the score flash up on the big screen and almost did a double-take.

93.30.

Wow.

That was huge given I knew I had so much more up my sleeve for my second run – we're talking two major, big-scoring tricks.

Clearly the level of competition wasn't as high as some events, which is why the judges were handing out higher scores, but I wasn't complaining. As I made my way off to the side of the track, I walked past Daniel Dhers. He was waiting to have his next run and said something in my direction. I didn't catch it completely, but I thought he'd said, 'Watch my next run.'

There was a cockiness about the way he'd delivered it, and normally I wouldn't bite, but I got caught up in the moment and fired back: 'I've got so much more to do.'

'Let's see, because you better be ready for my run,' he replied.

Straightaway I was annoyed that I'd taken the bait and quickly tried to refocus on the things I could control. Normally at competitions I might look like I'm taking in my competitor's run, but in reality I'm not there. My brain is watching myself on my run, constantly going over what I had just performed and visualising what I had to do next.

But Dhers had clearly got under my skin, because I *did* pay attention to his second run. He was the third-last competitor, and I was still in the lead, which meant I was guaranteed an Olympic medal. The question was, which one would it be?

Dhers had come out of retirement for the Olympics and was always going to be my biggest threat. And it was obvious early that he was putting together a much better performance.

'*Fuck*,' I muttered to myself when he'd finished. I was pretty sure he would have gone past my score.

Next to me was American Justin Dowell, who'd earlier crashed out in both of his runs. He was going off over Dhers's routine.

'That's the winning run! That's the fucking winning run!' Dowell screamed. I was standing right next to him, and yet he was carrying on like an idiot about his mate's performance. 'That's the one, that's going to be the score to beat.'

Again, I couldn't help myself, calmly saying, 'Shut up, dude.'

I was starting to stress a bit, since Dhers told me he was going to produce a performance, and he'd done that. Now I had to do the same. I was going to have to . . . *Hang on.*

Dhers's score flashed up on the scoreboard: 92.05.

I shuffled away from where I'd been standing and quietly celebrated with myself: '*Yessssssssss.*'

There was still one more rider to go, and it was the youngest in the field – Japan's Rim Nakamura – so I knew I had to try and stay focused. Anything can happen in sport. I was desperately trying to get my head back where it needed to be.

I'd never won a contest before where my second run was a non-event. In most contests, you did your two runs and then the winner was announced – sometimes it was the average of the two runs – but with live scoring like in Tokyo, you knew where you stood after each run. Suddenly my theory about staying in my own head and not watching my competitor went out the window, because I was certainly watching Rim's every move.

Then I saw it. A bobble. He'd done it on the box run, and if I'd seen it, so had the judges. When he finished, I knew I was the Olympic gold medallist.

'He's not beating me,' I said to no-one in particular.

Even then the other side of my brain was kicking in, telling me to focus on my second run as I made my way up to the starting position.

I was actually going over the routine I had planned when Rim's score flashed on the screen: 85.10.

I'd done it.

The crowd started cheering and I raised both my arms in a victory salute. This second run was going to be seriously fun now. I didn't consider *not* doing it, even though I'd already won, because in the weird way my mind works and how I push myself, I thought it would be cool to have the best score and the second best score of the Olympics.

I was going to put on a show. I was almost laughing as I dropped in and happily gave the crowd what they were wanting: a perfect front bike flip. It was like I was gliding around, soaking up the moment, but when my foot slipped off the pedal slightly when landing the opposite triple-tailwhip – which I'd nailed in the first run – I knew it was time to celebrate properly.

I pulled up on top of the box jump and saluted the crowd. Then, as I rode off the course, I had to wipe away a couple of tears. The emotions that had been bottled up over the four years since I'd heard BMX freestyle was becoming an Olympic sport were starting to pour out.

There had been a live stream set up for the riders, with vision of family and friends on the screen. I'd elected not to look at it after the first round, but now those tears in my eyes started overflowing as Kim and Noah rushed at the screen.

My wife was screaming at the small screen while the rest of my family, including my parents and brother, were waving in the background. All of the dedication, all of the sacrifices – it was all worth it in that moment as my little boy smiled at his dad.

It was only a brief chat, as I was whisked away for a couple of quick media interviews before returning to the course, this time without my bike. I'd quickly put on my Australian jacket and tracksuit to look the part for the formalities, plus the team face mask, which was an obligatory fashion accessory in these COVID times.

There was a small podium placed in front of the Olympic rings. Great Britain's Declan Brooks, who'd had that horrible crash at the world championships, was presented with the bronze medal first, with Dhers then getting the silver.

We shared a special moment, just before the ceremony. Everything that had gone on in the past was forgotten and we hugged it out.

'Look, man,' I said. 'I'm stoked that you came second and got a medal, because it's a true testament to the length of your career. I truly look up to you for having the career for as long as you have and for putting in all the work that you have.'

He appreciated my words and, given how he'd been a constant figure throughout my career – and even though we hadn't spoken for most of it – something felt right about us being together on the Olympic dais.

The COVID protocols meant we put the medal around our own neck, and straightaway I was surprised at how big and heavy the Olympic gold medal was. I couldn't stop looking at it as I raised my arms in another victory salute.

Then it hit me. I'd been here before. I'd pictured this exact moment on the bus.

ANDY BUCKWORTH

Australian BMX rider

Best mate

The first kind of interaction I had with Logan, I was in America and he and Kyle Baldock filmed a group web video for YouTube. It wasn't anything to do with the Olympics – this was before the Olympics were even a possibility for BMX – but the title of the video was 'Training for the Olympics'. It was just them riding in synch, like synchronised swimmers do. They posted it as a joke – training for the Olympics because they were riding together. I remember seeing that video, my first view of Logan, and then shortly after that I was back in Australia. We visited the Gold Coast for a Nitro Circus show, and I went to GC Compound for the first time. Kyle and Logan were there. As a professional BMX rider myself and in my younger days, everything was very competitive. I remember looking at this really young kid and thinking, *Holy shit, everything is going to change. He's coming and he's coming fast for everybody.*

That was even before Kyle blew up on the scene as well. Kyle was already making a bit of a name for himself, riding for MirraCo and just starting to travel. Logan hadn't even spent his first year in America yet, hadn't won anything, but I remember seeing Logan and being like, *Holy shit, this is just like another Kyle. We are going to have to beat both of them – how is that going to be a thing?*

Then, getting to know Logan, it was clear he had a different mentality, a different attitude than anyone else. He was so humbled by his humble upbringing, so humbled by not growing up wealthy. There are so many funny stories about Logan. The first time I ever met him he was riding a borrowed bike, eating Vegemite, peanut butter and jam sandwiches at the skatepark while everyone else was off getting sushi and Nando's. Logan would just chow down on the sandwiches from home. He is riding in borrowed gear, and on a borrowed bike, but riding better than everybody. I was like, *Holy shit, this is kind of the coolest thing.* You take it for granted now, but when you see how far he has come and how far he took everything from such a humble upbring-ing, such humble beginnings, that's the awesome part about Logan.

Things progressed like crazy - he was just getting better and better overnight. Every day we would come back to the skatepark, and he would already be riding. The 'first to get there, last to leave' mentality - I think that's a recipe for greatness right there. Every day we would get to the skatepark and he would have a new trick, or he'd be leading the session and be so dominant.

I was riding for Jetpilot at the time, and I had a really good relationship with the team manager there - his name was Chris Apps. I could talk to Chris on a friendship level, and so I went to his offices in Helensvale on the Gold Coast. I sat with Chris and said, 'Hey, there's this kid at the skatepark with no sponsors, riding a borrowed bike, eating peanut butter and jam sandwiches, but, dude, he could really use some help. I think this kid is the future. I think this kid is going to be the next thing.' Chris, without even batting an eyelid, was like, 'Yep, cool. Let's put him on the program.' Then within days Logan had a meeting at the office, and he left with enough gear to clothe him for the rest of his life. It just started off as a product deal, and then quickly after that Chris saw the possibilities, saw the potential, and put him on a paid deal.

That was the beginning. It gave Logan the foot in the door to be able to afford to go to America. I introduced him to all the top pros who we were riding with every day. It was a bit of a rocky start for Logan. He came in with so much hype and ability that he kind of scared the top pros. I won't name names or throw anyone under the bus, but he wasn't really welcomed with the open arms you think he would be, because he was ready to start stealing titles. He was ready to start taking wins. People were scared. I could really see it.

It was a crazy time for me. I'd ruptured my spleen, so I wasn't riding. I was living with some of the top pros and watching their mentality towards Logan. It was kind of like, *Screw this kid, we've already got one Kyle Baldock – we don't need two.* In the beginning it was a hard thing for Logan because he did ride so similarly to Kyle. And Kyle was adored; everyone just loved him because he had an Australian super-upbeat mentality. He was loud; he always said the right things. And Kyle was already making a name for himself, winning the Dew Tour that year and getting second in dirt and winning the first stop – he was really making waves. And then Logan is right there doing all the same stuff.

The real birth of the Logan Martin we see today was when he took his brakes off and changed up his riding style a little bit. That's when he really became his own person. That's when he started dominating.

He had a run-in with some of the biggest names in the sport over some bullshit. There was that huge run-in with Daniel Dhers over the key to the warehouse – that in itself is such a crazy thing. The 'unwelcomeness' he felt in the very beginning, in a sense, is what drove him to prove a point. That first contest in France, that

Red Bull contest, he just dominated. No bad-mouthing, no shit-talk, no ban from the warehouse. *Nothing is going to stop me, I'm here and I'm here to stay.* And that's what's crazy – nothing could stop Logan. He was like a freight train on a mission.

Fast-forward a hundred years when the COVID thing happened, and I was stuck at his house ... I was literally stranded at his house, because they'd shut down airports, they'd shut down runways, they'd shut down cities and towns and everything so no-one could travel. Logan returned the favour ten-fold and let me stay at his house.

Dude, he does a five-hundred repetition workout in the morning, then he has the most dominant BMX session through the middle of the day, then he'll swim. Some days he'll even back it up with another five-hundred repetition workout. It's like, dude, this guy is an animal. There is no stopping this guy on every level. They say that pressure creates diamonds, well, the pressure Logan felt in those earlier years, whether financially or socially, all of that hardship – that's what created Logan Martin. The pressure he felt really created the diamond he has become.

He is so driven and so focused on the goal that nothing will stop him until he achieves it. I think the only thing that creates that kind of mentality is that pressure. I say that to people all the time. I say to the American riders, 'It's pretty easy for you to not succeed because you are in your country of citizenship. You go home to your parents. You get a job. You do whatever you need to do, but as a rider coming over from another country like Australia, we're living in America and travelling the world. There is no option other than to succeed. There's no running home to Mummy and Daddy, because we're in another country. There is no-one there to scrape us off the ground if we fail. Failure isn't an option for us because we've already put so much into it. You can see that with Logan.

I remember when Logan was starting to really make some money in the sport. This was after the sponsorship conversations. It was kind of like, you don't get taught this in school. You are making money; you have to pay tax. He was like, 'What do you mean? What does it mean?' You have to get yourself an accountant, and when he got this accountant he was paying zero tax somehow. I was like, dude, this is all going to come back and get you – when are you going to try and buy a property? When you're not paying tax, if you're not showing income, you will not be able to get a loan. So we were having all these kinds of adult conversations that you have with the next generation – stuff that I had to deal with because no-one ever teaches you anything and you're just supposed to figure it out along the way.

I was having those types of conversations with Logan, and he's one of those riders who listens. With so many other riders, or people in my life, I will pass along some advice, and instead of listening they kind of take offence to it. Kind of like, 'Shut up. I'll figure it out myself.' Logan was like a sponge, soaking in every bit of information that was being said to him. He was also soaking in every kind of shit-talk that was happening around him, and it just created this unstoppable person. Nothing sticks to him; it just runs off his back. His dominance is on another level.

Poor background, minimal schooling. I went to school in Australia, too – you don't learn how to write emails to bosses and companies. You don't learn how to pay taxes. You sit there and learn about the First and Second World War, and the First Fleet – then they send you off into the real world and you're supposed to figure out the rest for yourself. That was exactly the same for Logan. He was trying to embark down this BMX path without any kind of guidance. So he was coming to me for that kind of guidance, and I was happy to give it to him because I had made all the mistakes. I had learned all those lessons.

I watched him grow up. I wasn't intimidated by him taking over from me, because he was in a different league already. I knew that I would make my own path in this world, so I never got jealous of Logan. I never got mad at him. He was willing to work harder than anyone else – me included. And that is what has created the best rider in the world.

When the Olympics became a thing – knowing the Olympics as a whole, whether you are a runner or a swimmer or whatever – I just knew the amount of work it would take and the sacrifice required. Then, listening to a lot of stories about the BMX race guys who were coming from an Olympic background, it was so different to freestyle. I was like, that is just not for me – plus, Australia has Logan. It was almost like the person Logan had become *without* the Olympics somehow made him perfect *for* the Olympics. Logan was that person before the Olympics were even on the table. So when the Olympics were put on the table, it was like, 'Oh my God, there is no other person in the world who is more suited to this lifestyle, this amount of intensity and this amount of work needed to get to an Olympic gold.' I was like, 'Cool. Step back and let him do his thing. There's no stopping him, no beating him. And if each country only gets one rider, well, it's going to be Logan. Come hell or high water, it's going to be Logan.'

He was frustrated when Tokyo was postponed – he was upset, he was confused. He's the type of person who writes everything down. Everything is down to the letter. Everything is in order, even to the point where an alarm goes off and it's time to eat; an alarm goes off and it's time to sleep; an alarm goes off and it's time to work out. Everything is down to the minute, and he and Kim had even planned for the Olympics. They'd had their first baby, Noah, around the Olympics. They were planning their second baby around the Olympics.

Everything was based around the Olympics to the letter . . . and then it gets cancelled.

Obviously, for most people, that would throw them off, that would ruin them. It would be crippling, but Logan never, ever stopped. He never stopped. The thing we saw in the COVID period, in all walks of action sports, is that everyone kind of disappeared. They went into hibernation, they stopped posting, they stopped riding, they stopped travelling – they stopped everything. Then when competitions came back after COVID, it showed who *didn't* disappear – for example, Logan. He had kept doing five-hundred-repetition workouts, and he'd learned the most insane bag of tricks. He was the fittest rider in the whole world, so obviously we knew who was going to win gold at the Olympics.

I was back home in California when Tokyo happened, and we put it on the TV. We rode the backyard – I've got a skatepark in the backyard as well – and then, 'Oh, it's time – the Olympics are on.' We went inside, sat in the living room, and we already knew what was going to happen. We watched, and it was almost like . . . I don't know how to say this diplomatically. It was kind of like it took the wind out of our sails. It wasn't like watching an X Games, where you had no idea what was going on. Everything was so planned out, and we knew what everyone was going to do. Everyone had seen the skatepark a year in advance, so we sat down and it was like watching a movie you'd already seen. *Alright, Logan is going to win – wonder who's going to get second or third.* That was the vibe. It wasn't screaming at the TV like when the State of Origin is on. It was, *Oh, cool, Logan won; we knew that was going to happen, sweet.*

When he dropped in and completed that first run, I think a few people got Olympic jitters. That's what hindered people, but Logan was cool, calm and collected. He was like, *I was born for this.* I agree. I really think Logan was born to win the Olympics – he's got that kind of brain – and there he goes, drops in blindfolded with his hands tied behind his back, and he wins.

12

BRINGING IT HOME

It was madness.

In less than forty-eight hours I had 50,000 new followers on social media. Everyone wanted to know more about Logan from Logan – or the BMX dude who'd built a skatepark in his backyard.

From the moment I put the Olympic gold medal around my neck, my life had been crazy. I'd been ushered away for media interviews immediately, while my phone started going berserk with messages. I tried to answer a few on the bus back to the athletes' village as I constantly checked the medal that was still around my neck.

I wasn't expecting the reception I received when I walked into the entrance of the Australia house. There was a hang-out spot on the bottom floor where there was a coffee cart and large TV. It was packed with athletes, and they erupted in cheers the moment I entered. They were going crazy.

It was an epic moment, and one I wouldn't be forgetting anytime soon.

We were in a bubble, so I wasn't allowed to leave the athletes' village except the following day when I was driven to the official press conference building in another part of Tokyo. I was operating on a couple of hours of sleep – but not from any sort of wild partying. I was just catching up on all the messages of congratulations and getting my head around what had just happened.

I was well and truly still buzzing when Patty Mills, the captain of Australia's basketball team, the Boomers, and NBA star, made a beeline for me. We shook hands and he said how awesome it had been to watch me win the gold. (The Boomers would go on to win a medal of their own, a bronze – Australia's first in Olympic basketball.) It was one of many great moments I would remember from Tokyo, some of which I was being asked to recall already as I hopped from interview to interview. Kim was doing the same back home. A TV camera crew had arrived on the doorstep at 7 am, so she was doing live interviews at the same time I was. Her phone was blowing up with people wanting to contact me.

It's fair to say the lack of media exposure for BMX in Australia was no longer an issue, and that was something that meant a lot to me. I was already getting messages on social media from people saying they weren't sure if BMX belonged in the Olympics, but after watching it they thought it was amazing.

There were also plenty of parents making contact, saying their kids were building jumps in the yard because they'd watched the Games, or how they now wanted to get a BMX of their own. The main thing I wanted was to put BMX freestyle in the spotlight and show a different crowd what it was all about.

We didn't stick around in Tokyo, given the whole COVID situation, meaning Australian athletes were being quickly whisked away after their events to a quarantine facility in Darwin. It was a quick way to bring the buzz down, although Noah was doing his best to keep it going.

He was watching the YouTube footage of me on the dais, biting the gold medal, on repeat and would say, 'Daddy, bite the medal. Daddy, bite the medal.'

My email was blowing up as well, with people reaching out, throwing business opportunities and speaking engagements at me. It was a constant stream of communication, and if they couldn't get hold of me, they were tracking down Kim, who was acting as my secretary while I was still in quarantine.

I've never been more excited to board a plane than the one I did in Darwin, which was taking me to Brisbane, where Kim and Noah would pick me up. They weren't the only ones waiting for me at the airport, though, with TV news crews and people lined up clapping and cheering as the athletes walked through the exit doors. I had a special gift for Noah: an Olympic teddy bear that had my gold medal around its neck.

It was all a bit crazy, but when I finally had them both in my arms it made everything worthwhile. Noah loved playing with the medal, and as we crept away from the media pack, all I could think about was hiding away at home with my family.

That's all I was dreaming of as we turned into our estate . . . but those thoughts were quickly extinguished as I drove down our street and saw the crowd.

There were people everywhere, lined up with handmade signs, and they were going off as we pulled up the driveway. All of my family was there, and Kim and Noah had written a beautiful sign of their own, which was on the front fence: 'Our champ comes home today. We call him daddy.'

There was even a DJ booth set up, pumping out tunes. Kim had obviously let everyone know when I was coming home, and this was the community's response. It was incredible, and straightaway the Olympic vibe was back. I did the rounds, showing everyone the medal, and they all wanted to be in a photo with it. I was even getting asked for my signature.

The support was amazing, and I had a joke with the neighbours who'd been against the building of my skatepark. One of the troublemakers had actually moved out because of it, but the rest seemed far more chilled now that I was a gold medallist. It felt like a win for everyone.

It was an epic day, but there was one thing missing . . . a drink.

I hadn't had one in Tokyo, and I again refrained at my 'welcome home' party, but I owed one of my mates a beer and I decided it was time. Early in my career he was always into me about partying with him, but I'd always said, 'If I win an X Games gold medal, I'll come and have a drink with you.'

The problem was, when I won the X Games gold in 2018 I didn't follow through with it because I didn't feel like

I'd accomplished anything. I didn't feel like I'd reached the pinnacle – that was still a couple of years away with the Olympics on the horizon.

Now it was time to party. We picked out a pub in Burleigh Heads and headed down with a bunch of our friends. The last time I'd had a drink was at my wedding, and I was ready to celebrate the greatest moment of my career. Mum and Dad came over to babysit Noah, and we left at 1 pm. I told them we'd be back by early evening – 5 or 6 o'clock at the latest.

We got home at 11.

It's fair to say we got carried away, and we certainly made up for lost time with plenty of beer, cocktails and spirits consumed. We'd started with about forty people, and by the end it was a hardcore group of fifteen, telling old war stories and just having fun.

The one thing I hadn't missed was the hangovers. I actually thought I was fine when I first woke up, but as the day went on the worse I felt. There was so much going on that I couldn't afford to waste any more days recovering from drinking sessions, so my alcohol ban was back in place again. But another ban was lifted.

I went and got my first tattoo in four years.

It was special for a couple of reasons. The Olympic rings was the only coloured tattoo on my body, and we initially had some difficulty figuring out where to put them before settling on the back of my neck.

The amount of requests was out of control, with TV and radio wanting a piece of me, while businesses, schools and BMX clubs all around Australia were also keen to hear my story. I'd never received more mail in my life, with people sending printed out photos of me from the Olympics, requesting my signature on them and asking me to send them back in the return paid envelope they'd also provided. That was pretty cool because I'd never had anything like that happen to me before Tokyo.

I was humbled that my win had touched so many people and put BMX freestyle on the map. News had even reached Hollywood royalty, with Nicole Kidman reaching out. She had starred in the iconic Australian movie *BMX Bandits*, which was a crime comedy-action film released in 1983. It was actually her film debut, and she played a plucky teen who helps her two best pals, also bike-riding hotshots, turn the tables on a gang of bank robbers.

Nicole reached out on social media, posting a picture of her wearing a *BMX Bandits* T-shirt. Her message: 'From one BMX Bandit to another. Congratulations.'

To be honest, I've never seen the movie, and I still haven't, but I've promised Kim that we'll get around to it.

Comedian Kevin Hart and rapper Snoop Dogg hosted a TV show in the US called *Olympic Highlights*, where they would give their own unique take on the Tokyo Games. They pumped up my win, saying how much they liked BMX freestyle. My social media went berserk after that shout-out, and I was increasingly blown away by the pull of the Olympics.

There was a theme at my appearances, with a lot of the same questions being asked, like, 'Where do you see the sport in five years?'

If you'd asked me ten years ago if I could envisage BMX freestyle being an Olympic sport, I would have said there was no way.

As I've mentioned before, the future of the big tricks is all about the opposite way – doing everything in the opposite direction to how it is normally done. This is common in snowboarding, riding 'switch' and rotating both ways, and I've really ramped up that approach in recent years, since it will become the norm.

In a practical sense, there will be fewer and fewer secret tricks, where you turn up to a major championship and drop something completely new. I decided to let the rest of the world into my bag of tricks after the Olympics, posting on social media clips of the three big tricks that I'd had up my sleeve in Tokyo but didn't use. They were the double-flair, a 720-tailwhip to barspin and a completely opposite flairwhip.

Another popular question was about the neighbours' reaction to the backyard skatepark. And then there was the big one: 'How does a kid from Logan win an Olympic gold medal?'

This one was very simple to answer. My life motto is, 'Hard work beats talent when talent doesn't work hard.'

I wasn't the most talented BMX rider, but I was the one who worked the hardest. And that got me to where I am today . . . the first ever Olympic champion in BMX freestyle.

KIMBERLY MARTIN

Wife, and mother of Noah and Luna

When we met I had no idea at all what he did. I didn't really know that BMX was a sport. I followed skateboarding, so even watching him on YouTube I had no idea – I just thought he was Jack's friend. I did a bit of an Instagram search and realised he had quite a lot of followers. I figured he wouldn't notice my message, so we got my friend to ask Jack to message me, and when Logan flew back to Australia we caught up.

At the start I still didn't realise how good he actually was. The fact that he could do those tricks on the bike was cool to me, given I had a gymnastics knowledge – it was like doing gymnastic tricks on a bike. But I still didn't really understand his position in the BMX freestyle world. I guess it wasn't until he went away for his first comp and I watched it live that I saw the hype surrounding him.

I made the trip overseas to X Games 2017, where we met, and within a few months we moved in together. Because I followed skateboarding, I knew how big X Games was. For me, I was just excited to go and see Ryan Sheckler, so Logan had to put up with me being a fangirl for someone else. It was really good to see how serious Logan took his riding compared to other people, and it was also a good insight into his personality and his dedication to the sport.

From the very beginning I realised he was pretty strong-willed. I'd say, 'Let's go out for dinner,' and he'd have something on the next day and say, 'No, I have to train.' At the start it was a bit annoying. I used to go to bed late, wake up late. I wasn't a lazy person, but I would go out and do things that would go late into the night. That's just what I was like, but then I would stay at his house and go to bed at 8 pm and wake up at 6 am, and I thought, *This sucks*. It wasn't until I realised exactly where he sat in the sport that I came to understand and respect the way he lived his life with purpose. I realised the importance of his routines and why he had those guidelines surrounding own lifestyle.

I respect that he was able to choose that path. It can be hard not to be led astray when you're growing up surrounded by all that stuff in Logan City – there is always a right path and a wrong path that you can take. It takes a special person to persevere with the good path.

Growing up competing in a high-risk sport like gymnastics, I have seen athletes suffer bad accidents. So having that perspective, BMX freestyle doesn't scare me, because I know how to remain calm. My biggest fear surrounding injury is more how Logan might handle it mentally more so than the injury itself. How long is he going to need a break? How long will he need to get through it?

When the Olympics came on board, it was very exciting for him, but we just kept making sure he kept living his life and didn't obsess over it. We made sure he took each event as it came: *first I'm going to do these things, and the end goal is the Olympics.* It was more about living in the moment at events. He went to every event with a purpose – to win – regardless of whether the Olympics were in play or not. That was the approach we discussed, because that was the approach that has got him to where he is today. There was no point adding any extra pressure because of the Olympics.

The lack of recognition was hard for him. He'd go over to X Games and win a gold medal, and it wouldn't be on the news. But if some football team had done something it's everywhere. Nobody knew – nothing in the local newspaper, nothing on the TV. If it had been the swimming world championships, it would be on the news and people would know. It's a credit to him that he doesn't do it for the accolades He rides and competes for himself and the people around him. He knows there are people out there who know who he is and respect what he does regardless if it isn't in his hometown.

During COVID, Logan continued training as he was because things could change just as quickly as when we got locked down. He just focused through that period; it was obviously tough. He was home more often. He had spent long periods of time away from home during a lot of our relationship, so to have him home full time was good. But sometimes it wasn't good, because he was always wanting to be out and about. That's his personality – he's always ready to go. With any sports person like that, it's hard to be locked down for any period of time. You're not injured, but you still have to stay home.

I think he was stoked with how he performed at the world championships after such a long time without seeing anybody, putting down the hard work that he had spent time on during the lockdown period. I think that got him through the quarantine. He went over there and did exactly what he wanted to do – he got the world championship title back. It was a good high for him pre-Olympics, but it was also his first time being away from Noah for a while, at a period of his life where Noah understood that Dad was away. That was probably the hardest thing about that time for both of us.

With the Olympics, there was a lot of discussion from other athletes about making their bikes in special home-country colours – setting the helmet up differently, with green and gold; America doing red, white and blue, trying to represent the country more – but I didn't really see the point in that. When you go to get ready to compete for the day and pick up your helmet, and it has got great home-country colours on it, that's placing extra pressure on yourself to go out there and do it for your country. So just waking up and getting ready like you usually would, that was definitely helpful in Logan's preparation, staying level-headed and just treating the Olympics exactly how he would any other competition. At the end of the day, it really is just another competition.

When I was younger and training in gymnastics, from an early age I saw the pressure that came with preparing for the Olympics and how a lot of girls would break down because it was at the forefront of their minds every single day. We were twelve years old and the Olympics was another ten years away, so for me that was just crazy. The Olympics are *ten years away*, so why are you stressing? I think the fact Logan was able to treat it as just another competition benefited him and gave him an advantage.

In Tokyo, with the minimal time difference, we were able to have regular communication. I just told him to go out there, be your best, have fun and don't put extra pressure on yourself. All the same messages and same conversations: just do your best because your best is good enough. We were supposed to go to a viewing party with some of Logan's friends, but because of the lockdown we ended up just having family over at the house – his mum and dad, brother, my cousin and niece and nephews. It was chaotic because that same weekend I was meant to have my gymnastics team in a competition on the Sunday. So I was going to go to the competition, race to the viewing and then go back to the competition. But then the lockdown happened on Saturday night, so the competition was off.

With Logan's first run in the final, I definitely knew he had more to give. I knew there was every chance someone would put down a good run, but as people started having their second turn it became obvious the pressure was getting to some of them. It didn't seem like anyone could take out that first place. I was really proud of him, I knew he would go out there and try and do another run, even though he was coming in first, because that's in his character. I was a bit bummed when he slipped up, but he knew that he had won – the emotions of that, that's how your body works. The fact he was still able to go out there and show them a little bit more made me even more proud; he didn't just throw away the run. Even though there were no crowds, he still tried to show the world and Australia exactly what he can do and why he is the best.

The moment Logan won I started getting media phone calls for the next two hours. The phone wouldn't stop ringing; radio people wanted to chat to me; TV news turned up at my door unexpectedly. The next couple of days my phone kept going off with people wanting me to contact Logan to make sure he didn't sign any deals with other people. I had to put Noah in an extra day of day care, because it was overwhelming to be pregnant and have him as well as dealing with all the media. It was definitely stressful, and then when Logan came back home it was hard to find a balance, because he wanted to still train but had to deal with all the extra stuff, like luncheons and things we had to go to.

When I look at what he does and the fact he made it onto the Olympic team and won a gold medal – he has done that on his own for the majority of his career. The last two years he had a manager/coach/physio helping out, but to get as far as he did without any of that is quite impressive. Coming from a sport like gymnastics, where you had a coach yelling at you 24/7 – when to train, when to get up, when to eat – for Logan to just do that on his own, sometimes going to training sessions by himself, I just think it's amazing.

The boys who ride obviously enjoy it, because they are out there doing it for themselves. The fact there are managers and coaches on board now but they are still allowed to keep doing what they were doing before is really good. It obviously takes a strong-minded person to be involved in that sort of sport, because there is a lot of expectation you place on yourself to show up – it's not anyone else making you.

14*

EVERYTHING YOU NEED TO KNOW ABOUT BEING AN OLYMPIC BMX FREESTYLE CHAMPION

BODY

Generally, the lighter you are, the better you'll perform at BMX freestyle. I have moved between 70 and 75kg for most of my career, and I was at 75kg in Tokyo. (The bike weighs 9kg.)

Some of the bigger guys are very good, but if you're too big it impacts on your stamina, which is the key. You need to have a lot of juice in your legs, a lot of energy, because every single ramp you're hitting, you're essentially doing half a squat to gain speed for the ramp. You have to maintain that level of exertion for a minute straight, while also performing your biggest tricks.

---

* Because I don't do 13.

That takes a lot out of you physically, which is where bodyweight comes into it. Another factor here is holding your breath in the air, which a lot of people do when they're pulling out their biggest tricks. This also uses energy and adds to the degree of difficulty.

You don't want to be focusing on your breathing at the same time that you're focusing on a big trick; but the more relaxed and comfortable you can be with your big tricks, the more natural breathing comes. Over time I've learned to breathe when I'm doing a big trick, which no doubt helps with my energy reserves at the end of the sixty seconds.

This breath awareness has all come later in my career. When you first start, your focus is understandably on nailing the trick itself, but I was finding that I'd get quickly fatigued towards the end of the run. That's why I started to focus on my breathing. It's not something many others worried about, but I looked at every little thing that was going to help me be better. Conserving energy by breathing properly has definitely been a factor in my success.

DIET

I've never been over-the-top in terms of weighing food or having lists of what food I can and can't eat or focusing on specific mealtimes, but I have developed over the years a regular routine that works for me. Back in the day at the GC Compound, we'd hit up McDonald's every day in between sessions before I realised things had to change.

The first step was a basic one: I just started eating food that wouldn't make me feel sick in the stomach. Initially, that was changing from Macca's to Subway, and then I started to learn about processed food and what I needed to steer away from. Limiting sugary drinks was also a big step, with Coca-Cola being completely stamped out from when I was young. While I did indulge in energy drinks because of my sponsorship, I have limited them more nowadays.

I do have a sweet tooth, which makes things interesting. What works for me is not buying sweets in the first place, because if it's in the house then I'll eat it. I do like to indulge after a win and maybe have a small dessert on the plane home.

There are periods usually when, leading up to a major competition, I might get into a hardcore eight-week block and focus on the little things. For example, I won't put barbecue sauce on my food to avoid the excess sugar. You hear elite athletes talking about doing the 'one-percenters'; that sort of detail is my little one-percenter.

My daily food intake looks something like this:

Breakfast: Cup of porridge with a scoop of protein powder, banana and peanut butter. I'm also a big fan of avocado on toast, so it gets a gig in the rotation.

Mid-morning: Two sandwiches – one Vegemite, one honey and banana.

Lunch: I use a lot of Youfoodz microwavable meals for lunch and dinner, which are high in protein and carbohydrates. Usually I'll look at either meat, chicken or salmon with rice, and I'll also microwave up some frozen vegetables.

Afternoon: I snack on yogurt, crackers and cheese, or some kind of fruit.

Dinner: Another Youfoodz meal with vegetables.

Snack: On riding days I'll have a fruit smoothie after dinner, just to get the calories back in.

TRAINING

Structure is something I enjoy in my life. Much to Kim's frustration at times, I like to go to bed early, around 8 pm to 9 pm, although since we've had two kids you have to be more flexible. Sleep is very important to an athlete for recovery and performance, so it has been a priority.

I don't have any set times when I train, but generally it's mid-morning. What I am strict about is, if I have planned to do a training session, I never cancel if I'm not feeling great. I will force myself to do that session because there is no guarantee on competition day that I'm going to be feeling a hundred per cent and on top of my game. Practising when I'm not at my peak is crucial.

My sessions usually go for between one-and-a-half to two hours, depending if I'm by myself or with a group. The way I like to ride is to practise all my bigger tricks every day, so I know they can be done under any circumstance, regardless of how I'm feeling or what the different weather conditions may be.

PADDING UP

There is a procedure I follow each time before training that borders into superstition territory. With my padding up,

I always put my knee pads on the same way: my right knee pad first and then the left one, repeating the right-then-left sequence with my ankle braces and shin pads.

I then put my jeans on before throwing a curveball into the routine: I always put my left shoe on before my right. It's all a bit random, but it's just something I realised I was doing, so I figured I might as well keep the pattern the same.

CLOTHES

BMX athletes can wear whatever they want, but depending on the weather conditions I like to ride in a singlet. But if I feel good in a T-shirt, I'll go with that. I'm not as superstitious about that part of my gear. At the Olympics it was all about the singlet, given how hot it was.

The jeans have to be skinny and stretchy. You don't want them to be stiff when you're moving your legs, given you're already wearing knee and shin pads. If pants are too baggy, they can get caught in your chain. When Australian Cycling came on board, they tried to get us to wear lighter, airy pants – almost like tracksuit pants – but they were too baggy. I tried them on once and told them straightaway that I wouldn't be wearing them. I've been wearing jeans riding my BMX since I was twelve, so I wasn't going to go changing that three months out from the Olympics.

I wear gloves with full fingers and have a sponsor in FIST Handwear. There's no padding on them, so they're essentially for grip, since my hands sweat a lot. Some guys will rub their hands in the dirt before dropping in, while others don't even wear gloves. FIST brings out new designs every few months, and they have some signature gloves based on my leg tattoo designs and my love of horror movies. There is also a replica of the Australian gloves I wore in Tokyo. My love of avocado gets a run on them as well.

I like to wear Vans. They're comfortable, and for a long time when I was younger I would go with the high-top shoe for more ankle support. I've since moved down to a medium-rise shoe – a Vans Half Cab, which isn't as bulky.

HELMET

The lighter the better here. I only wear a half-hat, which has straps under your chin and sits on your head just above your ears like a hat. They have to be certified helmets to ride in events. I very much enforce wearing a helmet because it has protected me many times, and everyone riding BMX needs to have the right headgear.

HOW TO BECOME A COMPETITION RIDER

There are different disciplines within freestyle BMX, so deciding which one suits you is the first decision. I am a skatepark rider who also rides dirt, and these are some tricks that are required in those disciplines to become a competition rider.

The tailwhip: You hold onto the handlebars and your bike will spin around in a 360-degree motion. Your bars won't turn – you hold onto them – and it's the bike that will rotate. You take one foot off and kick it, then the other foot comes off. You use your hands in a circular motion to get the momentum going.

The barspin: This is the opposite of a tailwhip. You stay on the bike, and only the handlebars will spin around in a 360-degree motion. My hand comes off and follows the handlebars around.

The backflip: The secret here is commitment. If you are going up the ramp, you are already pretty much halfway upside down, so you've just got to know how to jump. If you look back and bring your hands to your chest, you create the flipping motion. The ramp is there to support that rotation, so this is where the commitment comes in. It really isn't a hard trick, but it's just scary because you are fully inverted. Once you get over the fear and go all-in, you can learn in foam pits, if there is a facility close to you. It's a much safer environment. I learned the backflip on a scooter first, onto a bed mattress.

The 360: This is performed exactly the same way as a backflip, but you're going around horizontally, not upside down. You jump out of the ramp and do a full rotation with your bike – it is the same degree of rotation, just a different axis. The 360 is easier to learn than a backflip because you can work up to it, doing it out of a ramp onto what we call the fly-out, which is just a flat platform. You can start by landing sideways – a 90-degree spin – then progress to 180s. You can also learn by doing 180s and adding a half-cab, so that you're facing forward again. Then move on to a 270, working up to it with different degrees. The final step is completing the full 360-rotation so you can ride forward again.

Timing: The above tricks are very common. You then start combining them together to add creativity and raise the level of difficulty. For example, do a 360 with a tailwhip, then try a double-tailwhip. It's all about progression, but the main thing about perfecting a trick is the take-off, which all comes down to timing. If you try to spin too early on the take-off, you can either clip your back wheel on the lip of the ramp, or you can fully mess up if you miss your back wheel and accidentally slow your rotation. It took a while for me to understand that it's not about how quickly I complete the elements of the trick at the start – it's about the timing on take-off. It's also not a more-speed-the-better scenario, because if you have too much speed for a small box jump then you're going to clear the whole box. It's about perfecting the timing, depending on the trick.

The flipwhip: This is a backflip and a tailwhip in the one jump, and, again, the timing is crucial. Some people would think they have to flip really hard and whip really early to get back on the bike and complete the rotation. But you pop a normal backflip and, as you're taking off, that's when you kick the whip. It just cooperates better with gravity.

Pumping the transition: Every single ramp you go up, you are going to pump the transition to gain speed. You will pedal *at* the ramp, but you never pedal *up* the ramp. You stay flat-footed and then squat, do a half-squat pump into the transition, and at the right time you will push off the transition to get the height. If you have too much speed you can de-pump the transition and you won't push off – you'll do the opposite. When you land you want to be able to pump out of the transition as well and maintain speed. You can pedal if you need more speed for the next jump, but it's better if you land correctly and then pump out of the transition. That should ensure you have enough speed for the next jump.

Generally, you can ride a skatepark without pedalling, but it obviously depends on the layout. Let's say, if you land perfectly on a quarter-pipe, but there's too much flat bottom to just roll, you will have to pedal to keep that speed up. If you need more speed on a bigger trick then add some pedals, but I could go around my skatepark non-stop with no pedalling, just pumping.

Brakes: I used to only ever run with back brakes, with the lever on the left side of my handlebars. When I started on the professional scene, everyone ran with brakes, and then gradually people started to go without them. For probably my first eight years riding BMX I had brakes, but at the end of 2013 I experimented with getting rid of them as well. Sometimes you do a trick with brakes and you land with them semi-engaged, and it slows your momentum a little bit. Then you have to pedal to get your speed back up. I found myself relying on my brakes too much, so I decided after all the competitions were done that I'd take them off for two weeks. It was a very strange feeling, but I was determined to get a better feeling on my bike, get more bike control and get more comfortable not relying on my brakes.

In 2014 I still competed with brakes, but I was starting to feel a bit more confident with my bike. At the end of that year I did the same thing and took them off. Again, it was only going to be for two weeks, but I never put them back on. I was able to do every trick in my arsenal brakeless by the end of those two weeks. Everything felt better; my bike felt better. There was nothing in the way, no brake lever to grab on a barspin – things like that. Everything felt quicker – my bike felt quicker – so in 2015 I started competing brakeless.

Now it's pretty common to ride brakeless, maybe a fifty-fifty split among the professional guys. When I had brakes on I was a very similar rider to my mate Kyle Baldock, who I'd grown up riding with. I'd looked up to him, so naturally I wanted to ride like him. But once I took my brakes off I became my own rider. It gave me confidence to be myself and do my own thing, to concentrate on my own strengths.

MY THREE BIGGEST TRICKS

The key to pulling off any big trick is to feel like the bike is an extension of yourself. I try to be at one with my bike so that every movement is a natural one.

Switch triple-whip: This is a triple-whip but the opposite way. I practised this trick every day during the COVID period, but it took a couple of months for it to feel good. You have to make sure you pop the right way, have a certain amount of speed and that the bike is completely under you when doing the tailwhip. I did a normal triple-whip and a switch triple-whip in my winning world championships and Olympic runs.

1080: This is three full rotations with the bike over a jump. It is a trick that has been around for a long time, and many riders have won contests by pulling it out, so I perfected it.

Front bike flip: This is where the bike does a front flip while you're hovering over the top of it and catch back onto it once it's completed the rotation. You're completely off the bike. It's one of the wildest tricks I've done. There's not much control because it's all based on the way you let go of the bike. The timing of when you release the handlebars literally feels different every time. That's the reason I didn't really want to learn it initially, because to me it is an inconsistent trick, with too many variables. It comes down to hand–eye coordination, because when you are over the top of the bike you have to know when the handlebars are ready to be caught. If the bars are a little bit too far out in front, then you can't reach out and grab them, and you and the bike are in for a rough landing.

GLOSSARY

(PHOTOGRAPHY BY WAYNE CANT)

AMPLITUDE: The height of a jump.

BACKFLIP: Rotating upside down 360 degrees.

BACKFLIP TAILWHIPS: A backflip with a tailwhip.

BARREL ROLL BARSPIN: An off-axis backflip with a barspin.

BARSPIN: Holding the bike in position while spinning the bars 360 degrees.

BMX FREESTYLE: A discipline of BMX that includes any sort of trick riding or jumping.

BMX PARK: A bunch of different jumps/obstacles/features in one area.

BOX JUMP: A ramp with a flat deck on top and a landing ramp on the other side.

CASH ROLL: 360-degree rotation with a frontflip.

DIRT: A course consisting of jumps made from dirt, as opposed to concrete and wood skateparks.

DOUBLE-FLAIR: Two backflips with a 180-degree rotation, landing back on the same ramp.

DOUBLE-TAILWHIP TRANSFER: Two tailwhips travelling from one ramp to another.

DRIVEWAY BOX JUMP: The take-off and the landing have the same transition, with a deck on the top linking the two ramps together.

DROPPING IN: Riding down the ramp from a starting position.

FAKEY: Going backwards down the ramp.

FLAIR BARSPIN: A flair with a barspin.

FLY OUT: Jumping from the ramp and landing on the deck.

FRONT BIKE FLIP: The bike does a complete frontflip while the rider hovers over the top of it.

FRONTFLIP FLAIR: Frontflip with a 180-degree rotation, landing back on the ramp you took off from.

HALF-PIPE: Two transitioned quarter-pipes (a quarter of a circle) facing each other (making a half circle).

NO-HANDER: Taking both hands off the handle bars in flight.

OPPOSITE FLAIRWHIP: A flair with a tailwhip, all done in the opposite direction.

PUMPING THE TRANSITION: An action performed to increase or decrease speed.

QUAD-WHIP: Four tailwhips.

RESI: A landing that has a layer of foam and then a plastic material on top, making for a safer surface that you can still ride away on.

SPINE MINI-RAMP: Two halfpipes that back onto each other.

SWITCH TRIPLE-WHIP: Three tailwhips in the opposite direction in one jump.

TAILWHIP: Holding the handlebars but spinning the rest of the bike 360 degrees.

THE GAP: The space between one take-off ramp to another landing.

THE LINE: The route you take around the skatepark.

TRANSFER: Jumping from one ramp or feature to another.

TRANSITION: The curvature of a ramp.

TRIPLE-WHIP: Three tailwhips in one jump.

VERT WALL: A quarter-pipe that continues all the way until it reaches a vertical wall.

360: The bike and the rider do a 360-degree rotation.

540 FLAIR: A 540-degree rotation with a backflip, then landing back on the same ramp you took off from.

720 BARSPIN: Two full rotations with a barspin.

720 DOUBLE-WHIP: Two full rotations and two complete tailwhips.

1080: Three full spinning rotations with the bike.

1080 BARSPIN: Three full rotations with the bike, with a barspin in one of the rotations.

Off-axis 360 tailwhip

270 invert on dirt

Flairwhip

720 barspin transfer

The frontflip

360 no-hander

Frontflip no-hander

Flair downside tailwhip

CAREER RESULTS AND MILESTONES (SO FAR . . .)

2011

Free Flow Tour – Jaycee BMX Park Leg: 1st

Free Flow Tour Finals – BMX Park: 2nd

2012

FISE X Paris – BMX Spine: 1st

2013

Play BMX Contest – Park: 2nd

FISE Montpellier – BMX Park: 1st

FISE Montpellier – mini ramp: 2nd

Vital BMX Game of BIKE: 1st

NASS – Park: 1st

Big Air Triples – Miami: 3rd

Dew Tour: 13th

2014

FISE Montpellier – BMX Park: 1st

FISE Montpellier – BMX Air Spine: 3rd

FISE China – BMX Park: 1st

FISE Malaysia – BMX Park: 1st

FISE World Series: 3rd

BMX Cologne Superbowl: 2nd

FISE Xpérience Marseille: 1st

NASS – Park: 1st

NASS – Dirt: 3rd

Simple Session – Finals: 2nd

Baltic Games: 2nd

Dew Tour: 4th

2015

FISE World Series – Malaysia 1st; China 2nd; France 3rd.
   Overall Winner.

FISE Montpellier – BMX Spine Ramp: 2nd

FISE Montpellier – BMX Park: 3rd

Mongoose Jam – Dirt: 3rd

NASS – Park: 1st

NASS – Dirt: 3rd

SPX – BMX Big Air Triples: 1st

Recon Tour PRO at The Kitchen Park: 1st

2016

FISE Spine France: 1st

FISE Osijek – Park: 1st

Pannonian – Park: 1st

FISE Montpellier – BMX Park: 6th

FISE Denver – BMX Park: 6th

FISE Edmonton – Park: 1st

FISE Chengdu – Park: 1st

FISE World Series – Park: 1st

Nitro World Games – BMX Triple Hit: 2nd

X Games Austin – Park: 2nd

NASS – Park: 1st

2017

Monster Pannonian – BMX Park: 1st

UCI Urban Cycling World Championships – Park: 1st

X Games Minneapolis – Dirt: 2nd

X Games Minneapolis – Best Trick: 2nd

X Games Minneapolis – Park: 2nd

FISE Montpellier – Spine: 1st

FISE Montpellier – BMX Park: 1st

FISE Budapest – BMX Park demi finale: 21st

FISE Edmonton – BMX Park: 2nd

FISE Chengdu – BMX Park: 2nd

2018

X Games Minneapolis – Park: 1st

X Games Minneapolis – Dirt: 2nd

X Games Minneapolis – Best Trick: 2nd

FISE Montpellier – BMX Park: 2nd

FISE Edmonton – BMX Park: 1st

FISE World Cup: 6th

X Games Sydney – Dirt: 7th
Ultimate X Africa – Park: 2nd
Nitro World Games – Park: 1st

2019

FISE Saudi Arabia – BMX Park: 2nd
FISE Hiroshima – BMX Park: 3rd
FISE Montpellier World Cup – BMX Park: 3rd
FISE Chengdu World Cup – BMX Park: 4th
FISE World Cup – 2nd
Pannonian – BMX Park: 1st
X Games Minneapolis – Dirt: 1st
X Games Minneapolis – Park: 1st
X Games Minneapolis – Best Trick: 7th
World Urban Games – Park: 2nd
UCI Urban Cycling World Championships – Park: 2nd
Australian National BMX Freestyle Park Championships: 1st

2020

Chimera A-side: 3rd
Australian National BMX Freestyle Park Championships: 1st

2021

Australian National BMX Freestyle Park Championships: 1st
UCI Urban Cycling World Championships – Park: 1st
Tokyo 2020 Summer Olympics – Men's Cycling BMX
    Freestyle: Gold Medallist

2022

Oceania Championship: 1st
X Games Japan – Park: 1st
X Games Los Angeles – Park: 1st
X Games Lost Angeles – Dirt: 3rd
FISE Montpellier – Park: 2nd
FISE Belgium – Park: 2nd

ACKNOWLEDGEMENTS

I am humble in saying that my success has not come through my hard work and dedication alone. As the saying goes, 'Teamwork makes the dream work.' To my school teacher who asked me what I wanted to be when I grew up, and when I replied 'a professional BMX rider' said, 'no, a *real* job' – thank you for allowing me to prove you wrong. You were definitely not a part of my team!

However, I have had a lot of great support throughout my life and professional career, and many great people who took a chance on me at the very beginning, who have stuck by and helped me to be able to achieve and get to where I am today.

To my long-time sponsors, Rockstar Energy and Hyper BMX – I am grateful to have been given the opportunity to be a part of two amazing brands at such an early stage of my career. And I'm equally grateful that we have continued to grow together professionally and as friends over what has been a massive nine years.

To my sponsors past and present – I appreciate the support and opportunity to be able to represent your brands. Without your sponsorships it would not have been possible to put 110 per cent of my time and effort into BMX and make it a career.

To my agent, Lucas Mirtl – I told you so. Thank you for taking a chance on me when all I had to offer in the beginning was one sentence of self-belief: 'I just know I can win.' I am thankful to have had you come along with me on this journey from the very beginning, and for your friendship since day one.

Thanks to AusCycling for throwing Eric and Wade my way. Eric, you made me realise I have the bones of a fifty-year-old and can no longer bounce back without the appropriate recovery and rest. Through your knowledge, you provided me with a different perspective on what it is to be productive and remain at peak performance. I know that without you I would have run myself into the ground. Wade, I'm thankful for not only your umbrella-holding abilities but also the immense support and guidance you have provided me on a daily basis since you came on board. I appreciate the long hours you put in. You go above and beyond, not just for me, but for our sport: BMX freestyle.

To my parents, Donna and Sean – thank you for instilling in me what it means to work hard, for teaching me good morals and encouraging me to be a reliable person who is always professional and strives to be the best at whatever

I've had my heart set on. At the same time, you reminded me to be grateful and humble. It takes special parents to encourage and support a son who has dreams of riding a kid's bike!

To my brother, Nathan – if it wasn't for you I would have never been introduced to the skatepark scene. Thank you for being the big brother who always had my back when we were growing up!

To my amazing wife, Kimberly – I am certain your back constantly aches because you most definitely carry this team! I have so many things I'm thankful for that I don't even know where to start. Thank you for your endless support and for keeping me grounded. You are my definition of perfect, and I love you.

Thank you to the team at Penguin Random House who contributed to the completion and success of this book. My editor and publisher Brandon VanOver, cover designer Luke Causby, and everyone on the production, sales, marketing and publicity teams. Thanks to my mate Wayne Cant for all the spectacular photography you've captured over the years. And, importantly, thank you to Scott Gullan – it's been an absolute pleasure speaking with you over the past several months, and I am thankful for the way in which you have tied together my life stories.

Lastly, to my fans – I appreciate all the years of support. You have played a part in keeping me motivated and humble every step of the way.

Discover a
new favourite